DIVORCE IN VERMONT

UPDATED 2002

By Vermont Attorneys
Nicholas Hadden
Cynthia Broadfoot
with
John Pavese

ACORN HOUSE
Book Publishers
St. Albans, Vermont

Composition by Beckwith Bookworks.
Cover design by Hannus Design.
Cover art by Dave Sullivan.

UPDATED 2006

Copyright © 2003 by Acorn House

Library of Congress Control Number: 2006930964

ISBN 0-9745101-1-4

Printed in the United States of America

Publishing History
9 8 7 6 5 4 3 2

ACORN HOUSE
11 Lakemont Drive, St Albans, Vermont 05478
www.divorceinvermont.com

Acknowledgments

The authors wish to thank the following individuals for their help in completing *Divorce in Vermont*.

Susan Fay, Director, Vermont Family Court Mediation Program, for expanding and updating the mediation chapter and her overall support for Divorce in Vermont.

Lee Bryan, former Director, Mediation/Conflict Management Department of Woodbury College, for her assistance in reviewing the chapter on mediation, and the words of encouragement she gave to the entire project.

Judy Clark, attorney, for kindly contributing her expertise and enthusiasm for California law and clarifying the community property and domestic partnership statutes in the Golden State.

Jan Tyler, Ph.D., psychologist, who lent her invaluable experience to the challenging task of summarizing likely visitation schedules by age group.

Hy Steirman, for generously donating his editing and publishing assistance. He was more helpful than can be imagined.

Philip Gerbode, who was always there to encourage and support.

Contents

Introduction

This is not a touchy-feely book. It will not hold your hand and shed sympathetic tears. It certainly doesn't provide marriage counseling. Most importantly, it has no method or desire to prove that your spouse is a reprobate. Any therapeutic value comes from the comfort of finally understanding the divorce process.

The sooner you focus on the future and not the past the better for everyone, especially for you! The only ones who get rich from vengeance and spite are the lawyers. Vermont judges who sense it's all about revenge have no time for the individuals who revel in it or their attorneys.

Each state has its individual laws regarding divorce. Even when the laws are similar, how state courts apply and interpret those laws can be quite different. However, books on divorce typically fail to explain these differences.

Divorce in Vermont focuses only on Vermont. It explains the important issues you need to understand in order to make informed decisions. Make no mistake, this is a complicated procedure. So, as you move through the divorce process refer back to this book to regain your bearings and prepare both emotionally and logistically for the next steps.

Ironically, you will find that the same virtues that work to make a marriage successful are necessary to have a satisfactory divorce. Indeed, if both parties approach the divorce process with realistic expectations, a desire to understand their partner's point of view and a willingness to play fair, there is a good chance that a "livable" result can be reached without great pain.

However, if one or both of the players view the divorce as a vehicle for inflicting punishment or for gaining financially and/or emotionally at the expense of the other side then be prepared for a rough trip. In such cases there are no winners and losers, but only losers.

Now you're thinking, "That so and so who has made my marriage so miserable is going to make my divorce miserable too! How are we ever going to reach a peaceful agreement?" Well for one thing consider that you both have a lot more at stake in a divorce than in a marriage. In a marriage there is only the potential for disaster. In divorce disaster is a near term reality. So both sides better "get real" and quickly.

Use this book, also, to decide if you will be better off after divorce. Don't jump to the conclusion that divorce is the only answer. When children are involved both parents will likely see them less after the divorce than before. Perhaps quite a bit less. And then there are the financial obligations. Those commitments usually get worse following a divorce because there are now two separate households to support on essentially the same income. Remember that the greatest cause of poverty in the U.S. today is DIVORCE!

Sure your spouse drives you crazy, but marriage is only one of the ways to be miserable. Consider the fun of moving in with your parents because there is no place in

Burlington that you can afford to rent for your "bachelor pad". Or the equally pleasant experience of managing the house and kids all on your own while having to go out and get a full time job because the Vermont court says you should be working. And all the time raising the children on an orchestrated visitation schedule.

Finally, understand that whatever you decide to do, you will not be alone. There are nearly 3,000 divorces in Vermont every year. 50% of all marriages in the U.S. end in divorce. And for recent marriages the divorce figure is even higher. No doubt a lot more people consider divorce and decide not to proceed. Either way it's a decision only you can make. Only you know what you will be in for if your marriage continues. *Divorce in Vermont* shows what the way out looks like.

Authors' Note

A System Full of Humans

The problem with any legal system is that it is written by, used by and administrated by . . . human beings. That is as true in Vermont as it is anywhere else. Replace the judges, magistrates and lawyers with computers, make every spouse's needs and abilities the same and things become much simpler to plan and predict. But we all know nothing in life is that way. For sure divorce isn't like that.

This makes it hard to write a book giving specific information on a topic that is so variable. The only way to do it is to focus on what is usually the case. Unfortunately, the system doesn't work so it is done 80% of the time this way and 20% of the time this other way. More likely it is done 80% one way and 2% another way, and 6% another way and 4% another way, etc. until you make up that other 20%. Trying to list all the alternative possibilities is an endless task. Everyone would find it just too confusing.

The Most Good for the Most People

So, your situation may not always fit exactly into the examples and likely results given. This doesn't mean the book is wrong. It just means you are an exception.

When you see words like "usually," or "frequently," or "sometimes," or "often" before a statement your antenna should go up. We mean to say exactly that, it isn't "always" the case. Rather, it is only "frequently" the case, or whatever. If such a comment deals with a critical part of your divorce then it's a good issue to review with a lawyer.

That being said, everyone reading this book will come away knowing a lot more about his or her divorce. No matter what your situation, a good portion of it will fit into the book's discussion.

Lawyers, God Bless Them ... and Judges Too!

Part of the problem is that the law doesn't stand still. Attorneys are always out there trying to change the interpretation of the law. Hey, that's what you pay them to do. Does anyone want their lawyer to send them into a meat grinder when there may be a way around it?

Judges and magistrates, who are human as well, just add to the mix. We try to give you a likely outcome, but when it gets down to a certain judge on a certain day, well, nothing is certain. Anyway, the end result is that it all becomes kind of a moving target.

A Fairly Fair Process

Therefore, any couple who relies on a judge to decide the final terms of their divorce is taking the chance that the court will decide more favorably for the other side. The intention of the law is to treat everyone equally. However, "equally" isn't a clearly defined legal term in Vermont. What is equal to one judge may be different in the eyes of another.

This is especially true when it comes to assigning the physical custody of a child and to determining alimony. There are still some judges that have a traditional (you might call it old-fashioned) view of women and men in the family. Essentially they feel that women are inherently the primary caregivers and men are meant to be the primary providers. This viewpoint has resulted in decisions which by modern standards don't appear to be equal. Yet, they are rarely overturned if appealed.

Attitudes are changing, but it's a slow process. Men seeking a divorce today must recognize this reality. They may have greater downside risk regarding these two areas (physical custody and alimony) than do women. So, it's usually better for a man to make every effort to settle these matters before a trial than to roll the dice in court.

At the same time, this shouldn't encourage women to drag things into court if it can be avoided. There is more to a divorce than just these two items and predicting how the judge will decide on all the issues is just not possible.

Some Poetic License Taken

Each chapter gives examples of cases that demonstrate whatever point is trying to be made at the time. While these cases represent realistic situations, they do not refer to actual circumstances (except for the cases quoted in the Grounds for Divorce chapter). In other words, it's the usual "any similarity to persons and events living or dead is just a coincidence."

How to Act in Court

While the Family Court is a relatively new invention, many of its procedures are based on practices dating back hundreds of years. Some important ones are quite subtle and not necessarily covered in this book. The good intentions of people representing themselves are not always enough. Failure to understand courtroom etiquette can negatively affect how the judge views you and your point of view. Lawyers are trained to insure this doesn't happen.

However, we know that many readers will be in court without a lawyer. That's your right. It's also your responsibility to prepare yourself for this experience. Don't underestimate the importance of knowing the do's and don'ts of courtroom manners and protocol. Seek advice from those who are familiar with the process.

The Price You're Going to Pay

The fees and average charges mentioned in this book were current at the time of publication. However, we all are painfully aware that from gasoline to prescription medicines, and for everything in-between, prices are on the rise. So it's quite possible that these costs may be different from those you experience. Sorry!

Do Not Remove This Page Under Penalty of Law

If everything mentioned above looks a lot like a legal disclaimer, that's because it is.

We hope to provide a sense of direction regarding the divorce process and to make the reader sensitive to possibilities and consequences of which he or she may not be aware. Hopefully, this will reduce the surprises and save some aggravation and money. Of course the main goal is to reach a sound settlement.

But the legal environment is constantly changing. We strongly suggest consulting with a lawyer. A personal attorney is in the best position to understand the implications of your specific situation.

Can you do a divorce without a lawyer? Under the right conditions, absolutely. But you will need more information than is contained in this manuscript. Seek the help of mediators, councilors and state agencies. Many services are available at reduced cost for low income families.

This book will teach you a lot, but learning where the udders are doesn't necessarily mean you know how to milk the cow.

CHAPTER 1

Grounds for Divorce

Seven Ways to Leave Your Lover

Sometimes the only thing a married couple can agree on is that they should get divorced. Other times it's just another argument. One party may want to call it quits, while the other for good reason, or fright, or spite, will not let go. In Vermont there are seven different grounds that can be the basis for divorce.

1. When the couple has lived separate and apart for six consecutive months and at least one party believes that the marriage cannot be reconciled (called a "no fault"divorce).

2. For adultery on the part of either party.

3. When either party is sentenced to prison for either life or for three years or more.

4. For causing physical or mental abuse to the other party (referred to as "intolerable severity").

5. For desertion by either party.

6. For failing to financially support the other party.

7. If one of the parties becomes incurably insane.

A Quick History Lesson

A long time ago when most of Europe was of the Catholic faith and Vermont was completely unexplored all divorces had to be approved by the Pope. One day Henry VIII, the King of England, requested a divorce, but the Pope wouldn't agree. Kings don't like to be denied, so Henry created the Church of England. Freed from having to please the Pope, Henry promptly got his divorce. Thus, divorce began its movement away from being dominated by strict religious doctrine. (Apologies to the Catholic church, the Church of England and England in general for this abbreviated and probably somewhat inaccurate moment in history.)

By the time the U.S. became a fledgling nation the concept of divorce was even more advanced. It had become a legal issue with far fewer religious undertones. Vermont, like the other states, developed a number of grounds upon which a divorce would be granted (essentially all those listed above with the exception of no fault).

Still, the courts were not anxious to grant a divorce just because someone wanted one. Splitting up a family in the 1800's and early 1900's raised even greater financial concerns than it does today. What would happen to the divorced women and their children (not too many female corporate vice presidents back then)?

Since then, and particularly since World War II, the situation has changed dramatically. More women started to get jobs that allowed them to live independently. Some could even afford to raise a family as a single parent. Unfortunately, divorce laws were slow to adjust to this emerging "new world." There was still no simple way to get divorced.

Vermonters with money hopped a plane down to Mexico, the Dominican Republic or Haiti for a quickie divorce. Lawyers liked this approach as long as they got invited along to make sure things went smoothly. February and March were particularly attractive months for a tropical divorce.

But most couples in the Green Mountain State had to find a less expensive method to split up. In situations where both sides wanted the divorce, one of the partners would often admit to having committed some divorce-able fault such as mental abuse while the other partner played along. Sympathetic judges closed an eye to the game and granted the divorce.

Finally, in the 1970's, Vermont's legislature gave birth to the no fault divorce. An individual could finally get divorced simply because it was what he or she wanted. It quickly became the preferred way to go. Today about 95% of all divorces are based upon this no fault provision.

No Fault, or Six Months and You're Out

Vermont's no fault law only requires that the parties live apart for a period of at least six consecutive months. If minor children are involved then the divorce can be granted no sooner than six months from the date the divorce complaint is served (see the chapter outlining the divorce process for details). However, the divorce complaint can be served at any time. There's no need to wait for the six month separation period to be completed in order to get started with the court process.

At the end of the required period the court determines whether or not it is reasonable to assume that marital relations are still possible. This decision is usually based on what the parties tell the judge. Like so many things involving divorce the more the two sides cooperate the smoother, faster and less expensive is the process.

However, cooperation, while helpful, is not essential. No fault divorces cannot be contested. Only one spouse has to want a divorce in order to get one. No matter how compelling the desire of the other party is to save the marriage he or she will always lose. If either side tells the judge the marriage cannot be reconciled the divorce will be granted. An important benefit of this approach is that the focus shifts from placing the blame to structuring the most beneficial deal for everyone (especially the kids) in life after divorce.

There are a few things to keep in mind regarding the six months of separation. The first is that the months must be consecutive. Not two months in 1998 and four months in 2001. And the six months can include no temporary sexual reconciliations!

Most couples accomplish this by having one spouse move to a different address. However, some parties successfully demonstrate to the court that they lived separate lives for the entire six-month period while sharing the same roof. (Didn't Sonny and Cher do that for a while? Or was it Bill and Hillary?) Anyway, that being said, it's certainly easier to get through the divorce process if individual residences are maintained.

Since almost all divorces in Vermont are the no fault kind (even when there is fault), little time beyond this chapter is spent dealing with the other options (fault divorces).

What's the Point of the Other Six Grounds?

So, if no fault is such a great thing then why does anyone bother to use the other grounds for divorce? While there are a few exceptions, the main reason is revenge or anger or pure spite. They want the world to know that their husband or wife was a terrible person. "Hell, someone was at fault and it wasn't me!" Rarely is there a legal reason to do so and most lawyers will try to persuade their clients not to go down the fault divorce road.

For those in a hurry, admitting to adultery does avoid the six months of not living together built into the no fault process (but not the six month waiting period from the date of service if there are kids involved). The same is true for individuals having lengthy prison sentences. However, for a spouse to go to prison for three years in order to avoid a six month separation requirement does seem counterproductive.

Some people think that by proving their spouse committed adultery they will get a better financial deal than in a no fault settlement. This is usually not the case. Most Vermont judges recognize that adultery and similar marital problems are symptoms of a failing marriage. In other words, the marriage may have been over long before the affair took place.

However, sometimes the behavior of a spouse is so bad that it is worth mentioning to the court. One item considered by a judge determining the property settlement (division of assets) is called the "respective merits of the parties." If one of the parties repeatedly abused the other or was involved in serious criminal behavior or was continually unfaithful the judge may feel inclined to grant a greater portion of the marriage assets to the suffering spouse.

It's not necessary to file for a divorce on grounds of adultery, desertion, etc. in order to win this larger asset share. Your lawyer can make this argument and provide the necessary proof at the time the property settlement is being decided even if the divorce is going to be granted on a no fault basis (refer to the chapter on property settlement).

In fact, that is probably the best reason to understand the other little used grounds for divorce. While rarely the basis for a divorce, they do represent an argument to justify an improved settlement. However, many other issues also influence how the assets are handed out. Things like desertion and adultery are usually not the most important items.

The following descriptions include cases that are over 100 years old. That may sound outdated, but they are still quoted in the latest legal publications on divorce in Vermont. The more things change the more they stay the same.

Adultery,
or It Was Just One of Those Things

What is the definition of adultery? In the Green Mountain State adultery means "having sexual relations with a person other than one's spouse." Based on recent presidential history that's still a bit vague, but it's all the law gives us to go on. To get a definition of adultery that will work best for you just ask your husband or wife.

Once you know what adultery is, then you have to prove it happened. Surprisingly, the most popular method of doing this is by confession. Judges really hate for a spouse to go the private detective route with the sordid testimony, photographs, etc. Sure, it makes for interesting movies, but not in real life.

Besides, confessions are cheaper, quicker, and they avoid having the pictures become part of the public record. Adultery is not a crime in Vermont. The only benefit in proving that it happened, instead of getting a no fault divorce, is to possibly make your husband or wife uncomfortable.

Oh by the way, adultery committed by an insane person is not grounds for divorce. So stop saying your spouse is nuts. It will ruin your case!

A Spouse in Prison, or Doing Hard Time in the Big House

It's pretty easy to prove that your spouse is in prison. Under Vermont law if a marriage partner is committed to prison for life or for a period of at least three years the free party can petition for a divorce.

The criminal spouse must actually be confined at the time the divorce is requested. If he or she is still free while appealing a ten-year sentence, the other spouse can do nothing regarding a divorce (except on a no fault basis). If the same spouse waits until the jailed party is freed after serving only one year of a three-year sentence then he or she has missed the chance for a divorce under these grounds.

A fine point on the subject. There was a woman in Vermont who married a man convicted of second degree murder during the time he was free pending the results of the appeal process. It seems he lost the appeal and was given a life sentence. Once he went to jail the wife tried to divorce him (no fault did not exist in 1892). However, the court refused to grant the divorce because the wife knew when she got married that her new husband would very likely end up in prison for well over the three year period. It kind of takes the fun out of jailhouse romances.

Intolerable Severity, or The Pain Within and Without

The legal term "intolerable severity" stands for any type of persistent misconduct on the part of one spouse that results in, or threatens to cause, injury to the life, limb or health of the other spouse. Obviously, this covers any behavior resulting in serious physical injury to the innocent spouse—the classic wife or husband beating. However, it is not necessary to even touch the other spouse in order to be guilty of intolerable severity.

If the actions of one spouse cause serious mental distress, grief and worry on the part of the innocent spouse, that can also be considered a form of intolerable severity. Such actions can include threatening to do serious harm, displays of an uncontrollable temper, paying sexually focused attention to members of the opposite sex, and many similar things.

Now, don't think that losing sleep over something your spouse did the day before is sufficient grounds to obtain a divorce decree. In Vermont the court sets a very high standard that one must meet before a judge will make a determination of intolerable severity.

The acts of the offending spouse must be of such an aggravated nature that the health of the other spouse is certain to be threatened in the very short term. The court also demands that in order to reach this conclusion the facts and circumstances must be crystal clear so that no one could reasonably argue that damage to the innocent spouse's health will not occur.

One widely quoted case in Vermont involved a husband who had several indiscretions with other women and severely struck his wife twice during arguments over these events. The court felt the circumstances did threaten physical harm to the wife due to the grief and mental anguish she was suffering and granted a divorce based on the grounds of intolerable severity.

On the other hand, a divorce was denied in a Vermont case where the wife became tense, upset, and nervous with stomach pains and was "jumpy" due to the actions of her spouse. The court agreed that the wife was experiencing those emotional reactions. It simply did not feel that they were an immediate threat to her life or health. In short, those migraines you claim will drive you to an early grave 20 years from now just aren't enough.

Finally (and we really have beaten this one to death), it is not necessary for the actions of the misbehaving spouse to be directed at his or her marriage partner in order to prove intolerable severity. For example, a spouse who is abusive physically or mentally towards a third party like the children or a mother-in-law can easily create a mental anguish on the part of the innocent spouse which is health threatening.

Desertion, or Gone But Not Forgotten

In Vermont, if a husband or wife deserts a spouse for a continuous period of three years, the abandoned party can sue for divorce on grounds of desertion. That sounds pretty straightforward, but like everything in the law there are some important tests that have to be met.

The main hurdle is that the desertion must be without good reason. In one case a Vermont wife was sued for divorce because she refused to live with her spouse when he moved to a house "near his relations." Apparently, she had a good reason to desert him because the court refused to grant the divorce. That took place in 1856 and after about 150 years the logic still makes sense.

On the other hand, also some time ago, there was a case in Vermont where the husband turned to his bride as they walked down the aisle after just being married and said, "you go your way and I'll go mine." It seems that from that day forward he had nothing to do with her. Following three years of this "non-marriage" the court ruled that the wife was entitled to a divorce due to desertion.

Finally, if a spouse is missing for seven years and was not heard of during that time the court will grant a divorce to the remaining spouse. This may be desertion, or it may be due to some other reason, but seven years is a long time to wait for someone to show up.

Nonsupport,
or Pay Me Now or Pay Me Later

If one spouse and the children rely on the other spouse for financial support, the supporting spouse is obligated to provide such assistance if he or she can afford to do so. For instance, this could occur in situations where there is a stay at home mom raising the kids while the husband leaves the marital home and fails to send enough money to keep the family going.

However, the court is not blind to the circumstances surrounding a failure to pay. Two things have to be established. The first is that the necessary financial requirements of the needy spouse are not being met. The second is that the supporting spouse actually has the money to provide the required support.

The court will be looking for serious neglect and not just a tight budget. Also, the failure to provide suitable maintenance must be for a period of time and not just a missed payment now and then. Vague requirements like this point out the benefit of no fault. Now the stay at home parent can get immediate relief!

Incurable Insanity, or Crazy in Love

If none of the above six options have satisfied your situation there is still one more possibility. Vermont law allows for a divorce if your spouse is found to be incurably insane. However, the court will not grant a divorce on these grounds unless the insane spouse has been regularly confined to a mental institution for a period of at least five years. It is not acceptable to rely on a home diagnostic kit.

Summary, or This Way Out

At the end of the day no fault is the way to go.

CHAPTER 2

Vermont's Divorce Process

We Know What We're Doing and Other Smart Comments

Some of the information included in this chapter also appears in other sections of the book. It's worth repeating. If you don't get a solid understanding of what is being decided at each step, and by whom, the process will be overwhelming. Laying out the legal system in a single discussion (as in this chapter) combined with reminders of the process within chapters that discuss specific issues such as the ones on child support and spousal maintenance hopefully reinforces this understanding. After all, it's complicated. Law students get three years to figure it out. That's a lot more time than you have.

Another thing. This chapter focuses on the process related to obtaining a no fault divorce. As pointed out in the chapter on divorce grounds, the vast majority of divorces in Vermont are on this basis. If you are interested in using other grounds for obtaining a divorce some of the requirements will be different.

Finally, before getting into the details let's review the basics. In order to file for a divorce in Vermont at least one of the spouses has to have been a resident of the state for the most recent six month period. In order for the court to issue a final divorce order one of the spouses has to reside in the state for the previous twelve months.

Getting the Lowdown on Your Family Court

Divorce in Vermont revolves around the Family Court. While the Family Court seems to have been around forever, it's actually a relatively new development. Up through the 1980's divorces fell under the jurisdiction of Vermont's Superior Court. Getting divorces and most other things through the Superior Court was a very slow process.

The need to speed things up along with the desire to develop a softer, less businesslike style of justice, focused only on family issues, became the driving force for change. In 1989 legislation was passed to do just that and by the end of 1990 the Family Court system was underway with locations in every Vermont county. (See the list of Family Court addresses in the Appendix.)

In addition to handling divorces, other important responsibilities of the Family Court include juvenile issues such as children in need of care and supervision (CHINS), juvenile delinquency proceedings, family abuse proceedings such as restraining orders (the District Court still handles criminal abuse), paternity actions, and, most recently, civil union dissolutions.

The Family Court was built around the belief that a kinder, gentler system focused on family issues would simplify, and thereby speed up, the divorce process. In addition, the contentiousness so common between divorcing couples in the Superior Court might be reduced by the calming advice offered from experienced, caring Family Court judges. The end result was hoped to be a courtroom experience that, if not completely user friendly, at least did not add to the pain and conflict already being suffered by the Green Mountain citizens who ventured into it.

Well, it didn't work out quite that way. Judges found that many Vermonters did not want to have the seas calmed. They were out to get what they thought was their fair share and/or to wreak revenge and punishment on their soon to be ex-spouse. Also, individuals who went to court without a lawyer required lengthy explanations by the judges about the procedures. Things started to fall behind. Meanwhile, the rate of divorce was rapidly increasing and this further bogged things down.

For better or worse, the structure of this new court led to a significant growth in the number of post judgment orders. This meant that many more people were going back to the court after the final divorce order to have them revised. Anyway, in the end, the scale of arguments and delays in Family Court have shown only a modest improvement over the Superior Court.

None of this is to say that the Family Court is a failure. It just hasn't achieved some of its more lofty goals. A big benefit is that judges can focus totally on family issues. This allows them to become better trained and more experienced in family law. The quality of their work definitely reflects this expertise.

Also, the "softer" feeling of the court did calm some people down and in general the atmosphere improved when compared to the Superior Court.

Magistrates, Judges with a Mission

Another goal of the Family Court was to separate the child support decision from the other divorce issues. Closely tied to this objective was the need to get more uniform rules on how much child support to award. In fact, the federal government was insisting that this uniformity be established in order for Vermont to qualify for certain subsidies to its welfare system.

Prior to this time no child support guidelines existed in Vermont. Each judge determined what was appropriate. This resulted in wide differences in the amount of support being ordered under similar situations. It really depended on what judge was hearing the case, how good the lawyers were and what part of the state the hearing was held. Some orders were too much and others too little. Some were probably just right, but who knew?

So, the new Family Court structure included a magistrate whose only responsibility was to order child support. Indeed, the judge also has the power to decide child support at the final hearing, but only the magistrate can rule on the initial child support amount. If the judge feels that the child support amount needs to be adjusted based on other divorce issues covered by the final order the judge will usually request that it be reviewed by the magistrate in a separate hearing.

Very specific child support guidelines were established utilizing a formula that considered both the needs of the children and the incomes of the parties. This really limited the amount that support payments could vary from divorce to divorce when the situations were similar. Magistrates simply use the formula to come up with a payment amount. They can affect the support amount mostly by determining what data to input into the formula (see the chapters dealing with child support and income calculation). Magistrates also have some leeway to adjust the final support figure under limited circumstances (maintain current living standard, etc.)

As stated before, the Family Court continues to be burdened with too many cases and not enough time. Delays become a real problem when there is an urgent need to establish some kind of temporary support structure (both child and spousal support). In an attempt to deal with this overload, magistrates are frequently utilized to determine temporary spousal maintenance at the same time they are ruling on the initial child support question. However, their primary focus remains determining child support.

It Starts with a Complaint. So What's New?

Only a marriage partner can begin the divorce process. Divorce isn't a crime observed by a third party and reported to the police for prosecution. Criminal abuse of a child or spouse can be reported by anyone and, if proven to be true, the court (the District Court, not the Family Court) will punish the guilty. But even under those circumstances a judge cannot order a divorce. So if either spouse wants a divorce he or she must be the one to file a complaint. If both want a divorce they can flip a coin to decide who files. It makes no difference who initiates the filing on no fault grounds. They can even file a joint complaint, but that's rarely done.

The legal term "complaint" in most cases is misleading. In the days before no fault divorces the complaint frequently sounded like a real complaint.   The other spouse was accused of adultery or abuse or some other personality deficit. Today, about 95% of the complaints simply state that the parties have stopped living as husband and wife. No fault, no complaint. But it's called a complaint anyway.

Assuming the complaining spouse has a lawyer, the first step will be for the attorney to draw up the complaint. If the party making the complaint has no lawyer then the procedure is a little different. The complaining spouse must go to the Family Court (complaints can only be filed in a county where at least one of the spouses lives or owns property) and get a complaint form. After completing the form it's returned to the court clerk (currently the fee is $225 plus a small certified letter charge).

In either case, before the Family Court will take any action on a complaint, the filing party must demonstrate that his or her spouse was given notice of the divorce. The lawyer or the Family Court (if no lawyer is being used) is responsible for arranging to deliver the complaint to the other spouse.

Notice of the complaint is usually delivered by registered mail return receipt requested.   By signing the postal registration form at the time of delivery the spouse being notified is only indicating that notice has been received. He or she is not giving up any rights. No admission is being made. If the spouse being served has questions about accepting the documents an attorney should be contacted. In almost all cases the lawyer's advice will be to sign the receipt notice.

Sometimes the notice is sent by regular mail (so there is no return receipt) or it is hand delivered by the complaining spouse (if the divorcing parties have a good relationship). In these cases a form called "acceptance of service" is included with the complaint. The spouse being notified signs this form to indicate the notice was received and returns it to the other spouse's lawyer or to the Family Court.

Getting the Signature on the Dotted Line

Well that sounds pretty simple. Of course, at this point some spouses may not feel like being so cooperative. When the notice shows up for signature the spouse may simply refuse to sign. Or the complaining spouse may not know where the other spouse is living or working. Things can hit a snag right away.

First, let's deal with a spouse who will not sign. If you're the one initiating the complaint don't let it show up in your spouse's mailbox as a surprise. Discuss it in advance. Let him or her know what you are doing and the need for a signature. If you suspect that there might be a negative reaction to this request then deliver it (with care) in person. That's much better than letting it arrive coldly in the mail. But please, don't bring it over on your wedding anniversary or Valentines Day. Dropping it off at your mother-in-law's birthday party is a judgment call, but also not recommended.

The bottom line is that one spouse cannot stop the divorce from happening. Any attempt to stall the event will only result in higher legal fees and more inconvenience for everyone. In the end, the divorce will happen unless the one filing the complaint has a change of heart. It's far better for the other party to accept that fact and concentrate on getting the best deal possible on the way out.

Back to the task at hand. If the spouse being notified, after your best efforts, still refuses to accept and/or return a signed notice then you will need to have the local Sheriff, or similar official, make the delivery for you. This can be done at very little cost and eliminates the need for a signature by the other spouse. The Sheriff simply signs a court document saying that the complaint was served. Needless to say, at this point, things are not getting off on such a good foot, are they?

If the whereabouts of the spouse being notified are unknown, then the simplest method of notification is to publish the complaint in the classified section of the local newspaper for three weeks. Using fine print this will only take up a few inches of a single column. That is considered full notice and a legal substitute for a signature. Remember to get proof that it ran for the required time period.

The first key date in your divorce is when the complaint is served. The date that the return receipt or an acceptance of service is signed, or the day the Sheriff reports that service was made, or the date when the complaint has run in the newspaper for three weeks, is known as the date of service. Most time dependent requirements are measured from the date of service. For example, a divorce cannot be issued to a couple with minor children sooner than six months following this date.

The Anatomy of a Complaint

Complaints are publicly available. Generally, the entire court process, with the exception of some issues, is open to the public. But don't look for titillating tales of misadventure in the files where most complaints are kept. They are actually more like an application for a credit card. The following information is laid out in a complaint. If you have an appointment with a lawyer to initiate a complaint it makes sense to bring this information with you to the meeting.

1. Names of the parties.

2. Date of the marriage.

3. Date of the separation (when the couple stopped living as husband and wife).

4. Names and birth dates of all children under 18 years old.

5. Names and birth dates of any children 18 years old or older that are dependent due to physical or mental disabilities or are still in high school.

6. Description of assets (just a general list, with the large items such as real estate and automobiles broken out and smaller items like household furnishings lumped together).

7. List any legal actions that were ever brought by or against either family member (child or spousal abuse, guardianship, restraining orders, etc.). Include the date filed and the date resolved and the docket number.

8. Indicate if either party is receiving public assistance.

9. The addresses where the minor children have lived for the past five years (indicate the details of any court intervention or guardianships).

10. The grounds for divorce.

The complaint is signed by the complaining spouse and notarized under oath.

The Interim Order Is Triggered

Immediately upon submitting a complaint to the Family Court an interim order will be issued. While judges have their individual ways of crafting this document, they all end up saying that neither party can do any of the following things without first getting the agreement of the other spouse:

1. Cancel any health insurance

2. Cancel the utilities (gas, electricity, oil, etc.)

3. Leave Vermont permanently with the children

4. Change the beneficiary on any life insurance, wills, etc.

5. Sell or dispose of any assets

6. Take on any unusual debt (you can still buy the groceries at the Pricechopper with a credit card, but stay away from using it to charge a two carat diamond ring or that hand-engraved Smith and Wesson)

The purpose behind this order should be obvious. This is not a time to be making big changes that can affect the rights and property of the other spouse. Essentially, the court is trying to freeze the current situation, as much as possible, until the judge can oversee the splitting up of the marital estate and its members. However, sometimes these restrictions create a crisis and some flexibility is possible.

Once the complaint is delivered to the court (regardless of when the other spouse signs the notice) both parties lose some of their individual controlling rights to their property and even to their children. These rights are returned to them when the divorce is final. Of course, by then you may have only half your previous assets, and be seeing your kids on a scheduled basis. Whoever said life is always fair?

Pro Se Class for Those Flying Solo

About this time in the process, parties who are doing their divorce pro se (this means they do not have a lawyer and it is pronounced "pro say") are required to attend a training class on the divorce process. The one hour class provides a brief overview of the legal procedures and responsibilities common in all divorce cases. (There is a brief summary of the pro se process later on in this chapter.)

813, A Number to Remember

Nothing much gets done in the divorce process without each party completing a form 813. This financial affidavit includes an inventory of all assets and liabilities, as well as the party's income and monthly budget of living expenses. It is the cornerstone of all monetary decisions including those related to child support, alimony, and the division of assets. So before going any further in the process, now is the time you must complete this document. 813 forms are available from your lawyer, the Family Court and Vermont's legal Web site www.vermontjudiciary.org.

The Case Manager's Status Conference

Usually within 30 days of the complaint filing date, a Case Manager's Status Conference (shortened to CMSC) will be held in an office of the Family Court. The two parties and their lawyers (unless one or both are representing themselves) will attend (please don't bring along your kids). Representing the Family Court will be a clerk who has no decision making authority. The clerk is there to facilitate the discussion, find out what stipulations can be reached (see explanation on "stips" below) and/or whether hearings are needed. If all the important items are stipulated to at the CMSC then the hearings can be avoided.

The court is particularly interested to quickly learn what separation arrangements are in place. The reason for the rush is mainly out of concern for the welfare of the children in terms of custody and support. In addition to the kids, the spouse may also require maintenance payments right away. The court wants to be certain that no one (especially a child) suffers during the period before the final divorce order is issued.

So if a couple wants to make everyone happy and their own life much simpler they should show up at the CMSC with at least temporary agreement on the following (plus the completed form 813):

1. Child custody

2. Child visitation by the non-custodial spouse (remember to include holidays and vacations)

3. Child support to be contributed by each spouse

4. Spousal maintenance (alimony)

5. Living arrangements (who will stay in the marital home and who will live somewhere else)

6. Who will get the use of the car or which car if there is more than one

7. Who will have responsibility for any special payments such as mortgages, property taxes, utilities, car payments, credit cards, etc.

All the above arrangements are understood by the court to be temporary unless both sides want them to be permanent. Other chapters in this book discuss the benefits of appearing to be generous at this stage. The chapter on divorce strategies touches on the risks of being overly generous.

Let's just say that the court understands the difference between the long and short term. An example of this is a stay at home mom who needs money from the other spouse "right now" to live. Down the road the judge may figure that she should get a job and will either reduce or eliminate the maintenance payments as part of the final divorce order.

Anyway, whatever has been agreed to by the parties will be written up at the CMSC on a form called a stipulation ("stip" for short). Usually, there will be two of them. One will cover child custody and visitation and major issues involving property and debt. A second will deal only with child support. Sometimes an agreement called a discovery stipulation will indicate what information (financial, tax, property, business, etc.) one side must provide to the other side so "wish lists" can be developed.

Once signed by the parties the stips are submitted for review to the judge (spousal support, asset division, child custody and visitation, etc.) and the magistrate (child support). If there is already agreement (in a stipulation) on child custody and visitation the judge may not get involved at all. It will be left up to the magistrate to issue the temporary order (this is discussed later in the chapter) including spousal support, if appropriate, as part of his or her decision regarding child support.

Of course, you can show up at the CMSC with everything decided (permanently decided, not just temporarily worked out) down to who gets Aunt Martha's antique quilt. That's great. The clerk will have it all included in the stipulations. If the agreement is reasonable and the child support complies with at least the guidelines it will no doubt be approved by the judge and the magistrate. You will get your divorce as soon as the required time has passed. That's all there is to it.

Even better, avoid the CMSC altogether by submitting stipulations on all the required issues at the time the complaint is filed. The state of Vermont will be so delighted with your reasonableness that most of the initial filing fee gets refunded(total cost becomes $75). People and not the law make this a difficult process!

One last thing. If the parties have minor children the court clerk will give you a date to attend a COPE class (currently $40 per spouse). At this four hour session parents are taught how to help their children handle the changes and stress caused by divorce. It is mandatory that both parents go to this class, but it is not required that they go together. Don't get off on the wrong foot with the judge and magistrate by failing to show up.

Temporary and Child Support Hearings: Which Comes First?

A separate hearing with the magistrate is always held to decide child support unless it's avoided by stipulation. In fact, if only child support and spousal maintenance are in question (assuming child custody and visitation and other basic issues were agreed to at the CMSC) then usually a single hearing will be held, with the magistrate ruling on both issues. Extending the magistrate's authority in this way reduces the workload on the court and keeps things moving along.

However, if after the CMSC the parties still do not agree on the basics (child support, child custody/visitation, and spousal maintenance, general property and debt issues) then a temporary hearing with the judge must be held first to determine parental rights and responsibilities and parent-child contact (custody/visitation).

Obviously, child support can't be decided until the magistrate knows who will be the custodial parent and what will be the visitation rights of the non-custodial spouse. All this puts a lot of pressure on the court to act quickly to protect the welfare of the children. It should happen within 30 days, but usually takes longer.

Sometimes, there is an urgent issue to be decided and the temporary hearing is held before the CMSC. For example, there may be serious problems related to child custody/support or visitation. In these cases, if one party notifies the court of one or more urgent issues, the temporary hearing will occur right after the complaint is filed. (See the discussion on relief from abuse orders for information on the expedited process for handling dangerous abusive situations.)

Another reason for speeding things up is when the interim order (issued as soon as the complaint is filed) is causing an unreasonable hardship. One party might be in the process of selling a business and the interim order is restricting him or her from accepting a generous offer. Or substantial business funds have to be borrowed to keep out of bankruptcy. If the need is valid and timing is critical it's possible to expedite the temporary hearing.

Separation Agreement vs. the Temporary Order and Child Support

Most separation agreements (sometimes called a memorandum of understanding) are worked out between the two spouses either on their own or with the help of a mediator and/or their lawyers before the CMSC (often before even filing for divorce). If this is the case, the separation agreement is not a court order, but rather a contractual obligation.

It can cover as many issues as the parties desire, but it should at least deal with the seven items listed in the CMSC discussion above. That way, when the couple shows up for the CMSC the basics are already settled. The temporary and child support orders will probably end up being more or less identical to what was agreed in the separation agreement. Of course, this is always at the discretion of the judge and magistrate.

Regardless, once the temporary and child support orders are issued they override the separation agreement. Commitments in the separation agreement that are not covered by the temporary and child support orders remain valid.

Temporary and child support orders stay in place until superseded by another order or a revision. Couples who fail to reach agreement and leave it totally up to the judge and the magistrate to make these decisions take a big risk. If either spouse is unhappy with the results, he or she will usually be out of luck. These decisions are difficult to appeal. Even if circumstances permit an appeal, the process will often take longer than the time to get the divorce.

Remember, temporary orders are good only until the divorce is final, but child support orders are good forever (until the child is no longer eligible) unless revised due to a change in circumstances. If a significant event occurs (like you lose your job or the child becomes chronically ill or your former spouse wins the Power Ball lottery or the custodial parent moves a great distance away and visitation requires significant additional expense) it's possible to schedule a hearing with the magistrate to see if a change in child support payments is warranted.

If the parties want to insure a review of the initial child support order at the time the divorce is being finalized, they must designate on the initial child support order form that it is to be temporary. In this case, the court will automatically schedule a final child support hearing at the appropriate time. No motion is required to be filed and no change of circumstances needs to exist.

The Next Steps

Once the temporary order is issued the amount of additional work to be done is really up to the parties. If they have reached agreement on all the issues then it is just a matter of suffering through the required waiting period. This can be from as little as a day to no more than six months depending on the situation (see the time requirement discussion later on in this chapter).

Not surprisingly, at this point many couples will still have unsettled items and the best approach, as always, is to reach an understanding outside of the courtroom. How they go about doing this depends both on the issues being contested and the nature of the individuals. In the end, some kind of compromise is usually necessary and mediation can often be helpful.

If asset distribution is the question, it may first be necessary to get valuable items or properties appraised. There is no point in sitting down to discuss the distribution of assets if the parties don't agree on what things are worth. On the other hand, professional appraisals are costly. Make sure the appraisal expense is not more than the value you hope to gain.

Also, if a court battle appears to be inevitable this is the time to get ready for the final hearing. Child custody fights in particular take a lot of preparation. Statements need to be collected from individuals (doctors, teachers, therapists, neighbors, friends, relatives, etc.) who support the points of view of the respective parties.

Meanwhile, depending on who has what information, the opposing lawyers will certainly request data from the other side in order to present their case (the requests are called "interrogatories"). At least some of this was asked for in the discovery request during the CMSC.

Usually, these requests relate to financial and income statements, pension information and any relevant business properties. The opposing attorney is not only interested in the bottom line figures. He or she will rightfully demand all the details as well. This can create a lot of work and expense.

During this time it maybe necessary to have an additional CMSC and/or one or more SC's (status conferences conducted by the judge). SC's are often held to seek the judge's help to informally work out an issue that cannot be resolved between the parties. For example, one spouse wants certain documents, but the other spouse feels that preparing them is not worth the cost. Or the two spouses cannot agree on who should pay for certain repairs to a piece of property, etc.

SC's can also be used to get a "weather forecast" from the judge on how he or she might rule on a specific issue. This helps the parties understand how the court will decide if they fail to reach an out of court agreement regarding a certain item.

However, SC's take time to arrange and do not always result in the couple reaching a compromise. Some issues require prompt and definitive action by the court. For example, one spouse is not allowing the visitation rights specified in the temporary order, or visitation rights are being abused. In these cases an enforcement motion will be filed. Rather than an informal meeting like the SC, a motion hearing is conducted and the judge's ruling becomes an order rather than a suggestion. Please note that, despite the informality, on occasion a judge will issue an order at an SC too!

Finally the Final Hearing, or Here Comes the Judge

Once it's clear that some or all of the outstanding items cannot be resolved between the parties, a date for a final hearing should be requested. Lawyers may ask for a hearing date right after the CMSC in order to create some helpful pressure on the participants to settle the issues before the judge does it for them.

So, how long does it take to actually get in front of a judge? There is no straightforward answer. It would certainly be nice if the appropriate amount of time was blocked out on the judge's calendar at the time that the hearing date is requested, but that's not how it works.

Keep in mind that the Family Court has many responsibilities. This includes dealing with child abuse and domestic violence. These issues along with other serious matters often come up unexpectedly. Yet, they need to be resolved almost immediately. Sure, your divorce is important to you, but in the court's view, while all cases are important, divorce is not literally life and death. Some of these other situations clearly are.

Because it's so difficult to know when sudden events will demand immediate attention, the Family Court schedule only looks out eight weeks ahead. Some of the time in that eight week stretch will be left unscheduled in order to handle emergency cases. In addition, high priority cases that are not a surprise will also be scheduled. Whatever time is left is used to deal with divorces and other less time-critical issues.

It definitely can get worse. Divorce hearings are not scheduled strictly on a first come first served basis. Take a situation where a couple from Barre who cannot agree on anything requests a court date. They tell the clerk that one and a half days of court time are needed to present the entire case. Six weeks later a couple from Montpelier goes to the same clerk and also requests a court date. However, they have only one unresolved issue involving who will get to keep a desk of great sentimental value. They (or their lawyers) estimate that the case can be presented in 30 minutes.

Usually, the Montpelier parties will get to court well ahead of the Barre couple who might face a wait of many months (six months or more is not out of the question). It's simply much easier for the court to find a 30 minute window. The long cases (over half a day) will be stacked up on the side and little by little worked off.

Under special circumstances it's possible to speed up the process, but it takes a good reason. There was a case in which a divorcing Highgate Center woman wanted to move out of state with her children to be near an ailing parent. In order to do this she needed to get custody of the children so they could move with her. Complicating matters was her desire to get the kids registered for the rapidly approaching new school year. The court agreed to move up the court date in order to accommodate this situation.

It may also be possible to split things into two shorter hearings instead of one long one. This is called having "bifurcated proceedings" and it often allows things to move faster. Usually, child custody and visitation will be handled at one hearing and everything else at the other. If there is a requirement to take another look at the child support order, then a third hearing (this one with the magistrate) may be needed as well.

Without a doubt, the best situation is when there are no contested issues. These cases can be dealt with in a matter of days, if not just minutes. A quickly scheduled five minute court appearance is usually all that will be required if everything has been agreed to by stipulation. And even this court appearance can be avoided under certain circumstances if requested.

OK, Do It Yourself!

Still want to do a divorce on your own (pro se)? If the issues are not complex (hopefully there are no issues), then the process is not overly difficult. You or your spouse simply files for a divorce with the Family Court (forms and instructions can be obtained by calling the court clerk) and within thirty days attend the Case Manager's Status Conference. (Don't forget about the pro se classes discussed earlier.)

Assuming the easiest situation, at the CMSC the clerk is told that all items related to the divorce have been resolved. This includes child custody, alimony, child support/visitation, the division of assets and debt, and everything else. The clerk will fill out and file the stipulations as described above and the divorce will be subsequently granted. By the way, if everything (and we do mean everything) can be stipulated to at the time the complaint is filed then no CMSC is necessary.

However, it is not necessary that pro se parties agree to everything at the CMSC. Temporary arrangements for child support and spousal maintenance can be stipulated by the spouses or issued by the court while the couple goes off to work out the rest. These differences can be resolved privately between the parties or they can fight it out in court (just like they can if they have lawyers).

If things are very simple and everyone is in agreement on the settlement you can get away with doing it on your own. However, under those circumstances legal costs would be very low anyway. So, it might be comforting to have a little professional advice to ensure that nothing important is being overlooked. It's not necessarily up to the judge to point out such missed opportunities. Frankly, if the parties are in dispute over important matters the assistance of lawyers is highly recommended.

Minimum Time Requirements for a Divorce

A no fault divorce cannot be granted unless a couple has been living apart for at least six months. Usually, couples have not completed the full six months at the time of the CMSC meeting. If this is the case, then the divorce can be granted the day after the six month requirement is met. However, if they have been separated for six months at the time of the CMSC, and they are in agreement on all the settlement issues, then the divorce will likely be granted within the following few days.

The major exception is if children are involved. In this case, the divorce cannot be granted until six months following the service date of the complaint (see how important that date is). Some court procedures seem to make everyone (even if there are no children and the couple has already lived apart for six months) wait until six months after the service date to get divorced. You may need to delicately point this error out at the appropriate time.

In Vermont, a judge does not automatically approve all settlement proposals. If there are children involved the court will make sure that their needs are properly considered. Even without children, the agreement will be reviewed for reasonableness given the available marital resources. However, Vermont judges usually approve settlements that are mutually agreed to by the spouses, especially if both sides are represented by lawyers. The court assumes that the attorneys have protected the rights of their clients.

It Ain't Over Till It's Over

Even when the final divorce order is issued things may not be entirely over. As part of this order, the judge will indicate the date on which the divorce becomes absolute (meaning when it cannot be revised or nullified). The time between when the divorce is final and when it is absolute is referred to as the nisi (pronounced n'eye s'eye) period. The nisi period is normally 90 days. During this time it's possible to go back to the judge and point out an "error" in the order. Usually, such errors will relate to the division of assets or parent-child contact.

For example, the judge may have used an incorrect value on an asset, etc. Or the order may have failed to cover who gets the kids for Christmas. Also, the parties may finally realize that they can come up with some better arrangements than the judge did. Now is the time to get any changes they negotiate into the order.

Last but not least, during this time the couple may tell the court that they don't want to be divorced after all. The judge can cancel the divorce, just as if it never happened (which it didn't). One thing the parties cannot do is to marry someone else during the nisi period. They are still not divorced!!

An important issue affected by the nisi period is health insurance. If a spouse is covered by the health insurance policy of the other spouse, once they are absolutely divorced the indirectly insured spouse will lose his or her coverage. However, during the nisi period the coverage will continue. This gives the soon to be uninsured spouse time to find new medical coverage. Check on your rights and options to health care and health care insurance under Vermont law by calling the Health Care Administration's consumer assistance line at 1-800-631-7788.

The nisi period has been around a long time and in the old days there may have been reasons for it that no longer seem important. If both sides are anxious to get on with the "single's life" they can request that the nisi period be shortened or eliminated. If the judge approves, the nisi period will be adjusted with things becoming absolute on the day the nisi period expires. If it is completely waived, then the divorce becomes final and absolute on the same day.

Maybe It's Still Not Over

It's possible to appeal the final divorce order, but don't take the process lightly. First off, appeals are made to the Supreme Court and not the Family Court. There is a $225 filing fee and you will be expected to pay for a transcript of the court proceedings and a compilation of the original trial documents and exhibits. Appeals must be filed within 30 days of the judgment. Figure on it taking six to twelve months before the appeal will be reviewed by a three or five judge review panel. During that time the final order will be "stayed" (not enforced) except for alimony, child support and child custody.

An appeal is not another trial. New evidence can't be introduced. The final order will be over turned only if the original judge disregarded the law or demonstrated "abuse of discretion" (meaning that the judge's ruling, while not in violation of the law, was substantially unreasonable).

Indeed, appeals do succeed on a regular basis. However, successful ones generally rely on the appealing party having a solid understanding of the law. People can and do appeal final orders without using a lawyer, but that's a difficult row to hoe.

Is It Ever Really Over?

In most cases, divorce will not end the relationship with your spouse. It merely changes it. Depending on the complexity of the marriage in terms of length, money, assets and children it's possible that you will still be interacting for many, many years after the divorce becomes final.

The final divorce order itself is subject to revision as situations change over time. However, some items are more difficult to change than others.

The most difficult to alter is the division of assets (think of it as being etched in stone). Unless one side can show that the other party lied or intentionally withheld critical information about the existence or worth of certain valuables it is extremely hard to alter the property distribution once it's absolute (one vote for the nisi period!). This is why it's so important to know what your rights are to all assets before agreeing to a split. The court will not change things later on just because you made a bad deal!

Spousal maintenance payments (alimony) are more open to being adjusted in the future. Circumstances can develop that will make the original payments either inadequate or unreasonably high. It's also possible to get the length of time such payments are to be made changed. This is not an easy process, but the final order in this regard is definitely not written in cement.

The same is true for issues of child custody and visitation rights. Things change. The loving father who was getting the children 30% of the time has become a drug addict or a child abuser. If these accusations are proven in court, then changes to the visitation order can always be made.

By far the most flexible item is child support. This is merely written in the sand by the seashore. A little wind and water here or there and it can be entirely revised. By now you should realize that the number one priority in a Vermont divorce is the children. So don't be surprised if from time to time adjustments are required.

Divorce Is What You Make It

How complicated and miserable the divorce process becomes is entirely up to the two parties. It takes the effort of both sides to make it a reasonably bearable experience. It only requires one spouse to bring everything right down into the dirt.

But don't think for one minute that you can take your partner down while keeping your own feet clean. Frankly, that is one of the ways lawyers earn their keep. They are there to protect their client and if one side is going to act unreasonably, then the opposing lawyer's job is to make certain that it's an unsuccessful effort (and then get the court to have the troublemaking spouse pay all the extra legal fees).

Time and again this book stresses compromise. Things will most likely all end up at some reasonable conclusion no matter how long the journey. So why should either party see a benefit in trying to make the road a miserable one?

NOTE: See the summary of Vermont's divorce process, along with a flow chart diagram, in the Appendix.

CHAPTER 3

Finding and Using a Lawyer

"Lawyer" Is Not a Four-Letter Word

There's no question about it, you don't need a lawyer in order to get a divorce. Vermont law clearly provides for pro se representation (meaning representing yourself). However, the law isn't simpler and less sophisticated just because you're doing it alone. Not having an attorney means exactly what it sounds like. You better understand how to start and where to go and what to do.

Do you know the definition of marital assets and the rules governing their distribution? Is Social Security dealt with differently than a pension or 401(k)? What about assets acquired before the marriage or during the separation? How can you ensure getting adequate visitation rights for your children? How much alimony should you receive or pay? What if you are disabled?

The list of complex issues is a long one. Reading this book will help, but success depends mostly on your personal experience. What experience, you ask? Well, that's the point. Think about getting a lawyer.

Keep in mind that there's a lot at risk. The fallout from a divorce decree lasts a lifetime. It determines the quality of life that you and your children will enjoy (or not enjoy). It can mean the difference between living happily ever after or living with regret.

When the divorcing couple is wealthy the need for a lawyer seems more obvious. In fact, parties in a marriage operating on a tight budget usually have an even greater need for legal counsel.

The mother in St. Johnsbury raising three kids and working in a local factory can't afford to miss out on an extra few hundred dollars of monthly alimony. The father needs to be sure that something is left for him after the support payments are made and the assets split up (not to mention the child visitation rights, etc.).

Now compare that to the rich man's world. If one side overpays or under-receives a few hundred thousand dollars in a multimillion-dollar divorce settlement, life will still go on in a pretty nice way. So who needs a lawyer more, those with big incomes or those with modest ones?

Looking for a Rain Drop in the Sea

There are about 2,500 lawyers practicing in Vermont today. That's almost one lawyer for every 250 residents. However, not every attorney will be the right one for you.

Practice makes perfect whether it's a dentist doing root canals or a lawyer representing divorcing clients. So the first thing to look for is an attorney with a good portion of his or her practice focused on divorce work. The number of divorce cases a lawyer handles each year gives some indication of that focus.

However, don't rely only on the total number of divorces. An attorney who is involved in three or four big divorces a year may be more knowledgeable than a lawyer doing twenty simple ones. Use a little judgment. Good lawyers will clearly lay out their qualifications and let you know whether or not divorce is their "thing."

You may already have a relationship with a lawyer. Perhaps, one did some work for you regarding your business, the closing on your house, a will, or a family member's DUI arrest. The fact that an attorney was great at handling the refinancing of your auto body business doesn't necessarily qualify him or her to take on your divorce. Also, using a family lawyer who has a long-term relationship with one or both marriage partners may create at least an awkward situation and perhaps a conflict of interest.

Recommendations are a great way to enhance your search. They can come from friends and friends of friends. They can also come from other lawyers (including your family lawyer) who either do not do divorces or are too busy to take on your case. Just remember to look beyond the recommendation. Does the person making the recommendation understand your needs? If they used the lawyer for their divorce was it a situation similar to your own?

One way to check out how busy a prospective lawyer is with respect to divorce cases (also a good way to find additional prospects) is to look up their activities using the Internet. The court schedules for all Vermont lawyers are available under www.vermontjudiciary.org.

You will see exactly who is doing what in Family Court. There are also a number of other interesting items on this award winning Web site including a list of all Vermont lawyers, forms used by the court, answers to frequently asked questions and links to other helpful legal Web sites.

The final test will be when you actually sit down in the lawyer's office for your first meeting. If the meeting doesn't go well, don't hesitate to say "Thanks, but no thanks." It's far better to nip things in the bud rather than go on for many months before finally facing the fact that you're not a happy camper.

Many people wonder if it's better to hire a local lawyer with local knowledge (from St. Albans for a St. Albans divorce, for example) versus hiring a "big gun" from Burlington (all lawyers from Burlington think they're big guns). Well, the first thing to remember is that there are good lawyers everywhere in Vermont. Many simply prefer rural surroundings rather than life in the city.

Vermont judges rotate between the courts within a district. So it's likely that the Burlington lawyer and the one in St. Albans will both have had experience (and hopefully developed a good rapport) with whatever judge gets your case. Court clerks, however, don't rotate and this does give a slight advantage to the local attorney. A good relationship with these process facilitators can go a long way in making things move smoothly.

On a practical basis, the main reason for using a local attorney is cost. Lawyers charge for travel time at the same rate they charge for standing before the judge. If your attorney has to drive 30 miles to St. Albans from Burlington you will be paying for his or her time plus expenses.

Another important selection factor is compatibility. Divorces take time and involve many personal and emotional issues. Ask yourself if this attorney is someone that you can be open and honest with over the long term. He or she will be spending your money. Are you comfortable with that? There should be no doubt about matters of ethics or judgment. Do you get the feeling that he or she is a professional and a winner? If the answers to these questions are all positive and he or she has the right qualifications then you've found your legal representative.

Structuring Your Relationship and the Game Plan

Early on in the process develop a plan for using your lawyer. Of course there is the traditional way where the attorney does just about everything. This can work fine, but it has some drawbacks. The first is that it's the most expensive approach (see the discussion on costs below). It can also prolong the divorce process and may not result in the best final settlement.

At the start, your lawyer usually doesn't know you or your spouse very well. While an experienced attorney can get up the learning curve pretty quickly, he or she may never understand all the fine points of your marital relationship. How could anyone, except the parties to the marriage, know the hidden meanings in each other's body language and keywords? Who knows your spouse better than you do?

So, don't give up talking and negotiating with your spouse just because you have a lawyer. It's likely that the marriage partners can come up with better solutions to most issues than will their attorneys.

Of course, this assumes that both sides really want to find a fair solution. Frankly, if they don't (or one of the two doesn't), then it will not be surprising that the lawyers are unable to find one either. This inevitably leads to the worst case situation where everything is left up to the Family Court judge who doesn't know either of you from Adam. Then it all comes down to a six hour crapshoot in court (frequently less than six hours) that will decide how you live the rest of your life. Maybe you will get what you want and maybe not.

Remember, if you go into a divorce negotiation thinking you are going to gain and the other side is going to lose it will be a very long and painful process. Frankly, if both parties have good lawyers, they simply will not allow such a lopsided victory. So think of winning in terms of ending in a tie score. No one is delighted, but everyone survives.

A big exception to this discussion is if one party is being abused by the other. In this situation, the abused spouse is not in a position to represent him or herself in any discussions. The lawyers can work things out while the abused spouse looks forward to a life free from further torment.

It's Not Funny Money, Honey

In Vermont you can expect to pay a lawyer between $90 and $300 an hour for working on your divorce. Rates vary based on the location in the state and the experience of the lawyer (reflecting how busy he or she is). Most attorneys will be in the middle ($125 to $175) part of the range.

Typically, legal services are paid for in advance, but this doesn't mean the total cost is paid up front. Depending on the complexity of the divorce the amount collected after the first meeting will range from a few hundred to a few thousand dollars (called a retainer). As this money gets used up additional amounts will be requested in order to top up your account. Hopefully, a positive balance is maintained throughout the process.

Sometimes one spouse has access to significantly more money than the other. The "poor" spouse can ask the court to order the other party to pay some or all of the poor one's legal fees. Be sure to discuss this possibility with your lawyer.

Despite the jokes and "shark stories," lawyers do have a heart. Hourly rates have been known to be adjusted based on a client's ability to pay. Also, arrangements can be made to pay the costs over an extended period of time (even after the divorce). Of course, if you're getting a special deal the attorney will expect you to avoid running up the bill with unnecessary calls and unreasonable settlement demands that waste time and money by creating delays.

Dialing for Dollars

How easy is it to run up expenses? Well, consider the cost of a simple ten minute phone call. As mentioned before, many clients stop communicating directly with their spouse once a lawyer is obtained. They prefer to have their attorney do the talking for them. Your lawyer will not communicate directly with your spouse either. Instead, he or she will talk to your spouse's attorney who in turn talks to your spouse.

The costs generated by this approach are obvious. Lawyers generally have minimum charges for things like telephone calls and letters. In other words, if they make a telephone call on your behalf that takes 8 minutes they will usually charge a minimum of 12 or 15 minutes. Of course if it's a 20 minute call you'll pay for the full 20 minutes.

Since your lawyer is talking to your spouse's attorney (who will be charging your spouse for the same 12 or 15 minutes) you need to double the cost of the phone call. Following that call both attorneys will probably need to notify their clients of what was discussed. So add on the cost of two more phone calls. After the lawyers check with you and your spouse an additional phone call may be required between the two attorneys to finalize things.

And don't forget that an attorney will spend a few minutes writing up notes after each conversation. That's more money out of your pocket.

In the end, the cost to you and your spouse for these brief discussions could easily total an hour of legal fees. That might be as much as $170 or more! It would have cost nothing if you had talked about the issue directly with your spouse and it's far more likely that a resolution would have been reached.

However, there are situations where it is better to have the lawyers work things out. This is particularly true if the discussion involves points of law, structuring the agreement or the actual legal process of the divorce. Yet, so many things can be discussed directly between the parties. As you see, the price for failing to do so can be quite exhilarating.

By now you're probably thinking that while it's a good idea to have an attorney there is no way you can afford one. The miracle is that you probably can afford one. If both sides are cooperative and no issues are contested (please note the words "no issues") it's possible for the total cost per lawyer to be in the area of $750.

Remember that the lawyers have done this before. All the documents are in their computers just waiting for the blanks to be filled. Their assistants (who are charged out at a lower rate) know the routine and can do much of the work. The lawyers will address those areas that require their special training and expertise.

And the Final Bill Please

If divorces were not so painfully personal most of them could be completed with little effort. The old expressions, "You can't get blood from a stone" and "There's no free lunch" apply in spades when it comes to divorce. So in the end, settlements are generally fair to both sides. Unfortunately, bitterness, pettiness and pure illogical behavior can make the road leading to this reasonable conclusion a long and costly one.

Just how much a contested divorce costs is hard to say because there are so many variables. You can be certain that expenses rise rapidly anytime the parties disagree on an issue. For example, if they fail to settle on the value of a house and hire separate appraisers, the combined appraisal fees may be $400 to $600. If it's a commercial building each appraisal might cost $2,000 or more. Child custody fights can take on an economic life of their own (see the child custody chapter). Every additional issue becomes surrounded by dollar signs.

Even if there are only a few items in dispute you can expect an additional one to five thousand dollars for legal and service fees. If things really get out of hand it can cost as much as $100,000 for each side to cover the costs of lawyers and the other professionals involved in such matters. The sad part is that it only takes one unreasonable party to make these skyrocketing expenses unavoidable. Of course, if the couple lacks such lofty funds the incentive to compromise is great.

The good news is that the fees collected by the state of Vermont to process your divorce are relatively modest. They will total only about $225 for the entire ordeal.

One last thought on how to keep the cost down. If you can't work out a deal with your spouse on your own, try mediation. Mediation can be a lot less expensive than doing the "full monty" with two lawyers and much, much less costly than going to court. The lawyers still have a role to play, but it will require less of their expensive time (see the chapter on mediation).

The First Meeting with Your Lawyer

The first part of this chapter provided an overview for acquiring and using an attorney. Now let's get into the details as they relate to the initial meeting.

Making the first appointment to see a lawyer doesn't imply a final commitment. However, based on recommendations and reputation you should already be pretty confident that he or she is a good choice. Talking directly to the attorney when you call to set the meeting date will allow for a quick one on one evaluation. Ask about first meeting charges and the hourly rate so that there are no surprises. If you have a good reason for needing a break on the fees don't hesitate to mention it at the time of your telephone call. You might as well know right away whether or not the attorney is willing to consider an adjustment.

There are several different approaches to first meeting costs. While a few lawyers don't charge anything, most require some payment in order to make sure that the potential client is not just "window shopping." The amount can be a fixed fee ranging from $50 to as much as $200, or simply the hourly rate for however long the meeting lasts. Fixed fee meetings are definitely more relaxing since you don't have to keep one eye on your watch while wondering how much it's cost so far.

The initial meeting should last between one and two hours depending on the complexity of the divorce. Being prepared and organized can greatly reduce the time required and increase the productivity of the meeting. Strive to accomplish the following objectives:

1. *Evaluate the Lawyer.* Determine if you are satisfied with the lawyer's experience in handling divorces similar to your own situation. Are you compatible? How well will you be able to work together?

2. *Discuss the Issues.* You will need to give the lawyer a complete overview of the issues surrounding the divorce (see the meeting efficiency section below). Make note of the questions you can't answer on the spot and submit responses by telephone, e-mail or letter.

3. *Understand the Process.* The lawyer should outline the divorce process and review the legal rights of the parties. This will give you a sense of direction, timing and a general idea of the likely settlement terms.

4. *Develop the Game Plan.* Establish your objectives and work out a game plan to reach them. This includes deciding who will do what. Make sure

that you feel comfortable with how matters will proceed. While the attorney is an expert in the law, you know the situation best. This is the time to voice your opinions and concerns. Agree on what actions you will be notified about before they are taken by the lawyer (limits on spending, agreeing to meetings, telephone calls, etc.).

5. *Understand the Costs.* The lawyer should clearly lay out all the potential costs related to the divorce and the billing policy of the firm including the required retainer. Discuss the hourly rates charged for the lawyer and paralegal, the cost for copying documents, the minimum billing amounts for telephone calls and preparing letters, etc. Remember to address special payment requests you feel are necessary (fee reductions and/or credit).

6. *Agree on Proceeding.* By the end of the meeting the lawyer will decide to either take the case or suggest another option. Unless unexpected issues or a conflict of interest are revealed it's most likely that the attorney will take the case. However, if for some reason you are not satisfied there is nothing wrong in saying so. Remember, divorce is a growth industry. If the lawyer is good there will be other clients that make a better match.

Shortly after the meeting (assuming you agree to go forward) the lawyer will provide you with a document outlining all the issues agreed to at the first meeting, including a fee schedule, credit policy, the retainer, etc. It will also clearly state what you are paying the lawyer to do. In this case it will be to handle only your divorce. It may also say what the lawyer is not doing (for example, "the lawyer is not providing any tax advice").

Meeting Efficiency, or Getting the Most for Your Money

At your first meeting the lawyer will be like a computer searching for data. The attorney already has the operating software (the law, the legal process, how to present a case, etc.). Your job is to enter into this system all the facts related to your situation. But just like a computer, if you provide incorrect, incomplete or misleading data then you can't expect the results to be satisfactory. Eventually, it will get sorted out, but you will have added substantial expense to the processes. In addition, opportunities to get a better settlement may be lost.

So come to the initial meeting fully prepared. This is not the time to get carried away with bitterness or sarcasm about your spouse. Your attorney is looking for facts and events. All the emotional stuff just takes up valuable time. If you must cry on someone's shoulder try to do it with a friend who isn't charging you $150 an hour. Hey, it's your money.

At the initial meeting bring along the following written information:

1. The names, dates of birth, addresses/telephone numbers for you, your spouse and the children. Include a short biography of each member of the family in order to make the individuals come to life for the lawyer.

2. Copies of all relevant legal documents such as separation and prenuptial agreements, restraining orders, etc.

3. Any proposal or correspondence that you exchanged with your spouse regarding settlement issues.

4. Tax statements for the last three years and pay stubs for the last three months.

5. A list of all the major assets that you and your spouse possess. Indicate whose name each item is owned under and its estimated resale value (this value may be more or less than what you paid for them). Household furnishings can be lumped together under a single estimated value. And don't forget to put down how much money you owe on each item (indicate the monthly payments and how long before each will be paid off). Finally, list any other debt you have such as credit card balances, etc.

6. A time line of events covering all-important activities leading up to the decision to divorce. This is one of the best ways of getting your story across to the attorney. It is simply a list of key events in date order that are relevant to the divorce. Remember at this first meeting you are giving the lawyer a ton of data about a family he or she has never heard of before. The time line helps eliminate confusion and misunderstanding.

7. If you are the one filing the complaint don't forget to bring the information required to fill out a complaint form listed in the chapter on Vermont's divorce process.

The lawyer will take a lot of notes at the meeting and so should you. Get a binder or some other kind of filing system and keep all notes and documents in one place. If being organized is not your strength in day to day living try to make this an exception. After all, the divorce settlement is likely to have a tremendous impact on your relationship with your children, as well as possibly being the most important financial event of your life.

What about Sharing a Lawyer?

One lawyer cannot represent two opposing clients. So if just one lawyer is used, that attorney is representing only one of the parties and the other party has no representation. This works best when both sides have already reached a clear understanding on the settlement issues. Hopefully, there are no issues or in the worst case they are very simple ones.

For example, a couple in Manchester Center were married for a short time when they decided to separate. Never bothering to get divorced they lived apart for almost ten years. Then one day the husband decided to marry his girlfriend (more her decision than his), but first he needed a divorce.

He and his wife had been living successful and quite separate lives for a long time. Virtually all their assets were acquired after the separation. Best of all, there was no hostility between them. In fact, they enjoyed each other's company. The husband hired a lawyer who drew up a settlement agreement based on the desires of both parties. The wife signed the required documents prepared by his lawyer who then filed them with the court. The divorce was granted only a few days later. The ex-wife was invited to the couple's wedding.

In this case, the lawyer made it clear to the wife that he was only representing the husband. Such an approach required a good deal of trust on the part of the wife since she had little protection under the law if she made a bad deal. It would be unethical for the husband's attorney to advise her on what to do. The judge is also under no obligation to point out an opportunity the wife may be giving up by agreeing to the proposed settlement. In this particular divorce the results were quite satisfactory and the legal bills very low.

Keep in mind that we are talking about one side having a lawyer and one side having no lawyer. They are not sharing a lawyer. Divorcing parties can't share an attorney.

Changing Your Lawyer

Even when things look good at the start, along the way you may become unhappy with the lawyer you selected. There is no obligation to continue this relationship. However, making such a mid-stream change should only be done after careful consideration. Remember, new representation will not change the facts in your case. But, if you're not able to resolve the problem with your attorney, don't feel uncomfortable about making the change. Sometimes things just don't work out. On the other hand, a party who is into his or her third or fourth lawyer risks giving a poor impression to the judge.

So, Is a Lawyer Really Necessary?

Read this book and then decide if you need a lawyer. Remember, it's often a matter of "pay me now or pay me later." And it's far cheaper for someone to have an attorney work out a fair settlement before the divorce than to have him or her try to fix a bad decree.

Nevertheless, if you decide to handle your own divorce some key points in this chapter are still very useful. After all, you'll need to be as prepared as any lawyer would be if you expect to succeed.

1. Get all the details of your marriage organized properly (time line, asset valuation, debt details, legal and tax documents, etc.).

2. Keep detailed notes of all relevant conversations and proposals.

3. Try to settle things with your spouse out of court.

Finally, some people who wish to do a pro se (no lawyer) divorce will still employ a lawyer as a consultant for particular issues. Under this arrangement the attorney is only used to provide information on certain areas of the law and to review documents before signing, etc. Most of the work is done by the client. Depending on the complexity of the divorce and how well the parties are working together, this can be a satisfactory way of holding down the legal costs. Mediators often recommend this approach.

CHAPTER 4

Mediation

Mediators and What They Do

Many people confuse arbitration with mediation. Arbitrators hear a case and impose a settlement that the parties agree in advance will be legally binding. Mediators don't make any rulings or final decisions. Instead, they attempt to get the spouses to work out their own solution. Settlements are never forced upon the parties. This means that mediation may or may not resolve the problem. But it frequently does lead to a settlement.

The mediator's role is to create an atmosphere that reduces hostility and encourages understanding and compromise. Through the use of probing questions, role playing and similar techniques each party comes to better understand the desires of the other, as well as their own central needs. The objective in a divorce negotiation is to reach an agreement that is satisfying to both sides. Many couples find this difficult to achieve without a mediator's help.

Mediation can be particularly helpful when dealing with deeply emotional issues such as where the children will live, how and when the kids will see each parent and the grandparents, the process for making important decisions regarding schooling, healthcare, religion, etc. However, as good as it works for some folks it's not for everyone.

This is especially true in cases where a spouse has been mentally or physically abused by his or her partner. Abused individuals are simply unable to represent themselves against their abusers. Anyway, a person that abuses a spouse can rarely be trusted to live up to a mediated agreement.

Different Strokes for Different Folks

Couples doing a pro se divorce (using no lawyer) often rely on a mediator to help them arrive at a complete settlement. When lawyers are involved the parties may be more selective about their use of mediation. It depends on how enthusiastically their attorneys embrace the process and the desires of the spouses.

Pro se couples usually come to the mediation session with a reasonable amount of openness and flexibility. Their lack of a preconceived settlement makes it easier to find common ground. The negative side of this is that one or both spouses may be unaware or misinformed about important legal rights. Part of the mediator's responsibility is to insure that this shortcoming is appropriately addressed.

Just the opposite may be true for couples working with lawyers. The attorneys will have discussed with them their rights, possible settlement structures and likely court judgments if things are allowed to go that far. When these spouses show up at the mediation they may have some firm ideas regarding the final outcome.

While knowing your rights is important, a good settlement has to reflect more than what the law grants to
each party. It's possible for the spouses to achieve all
their "rights" and to still be unhappy with the final outcome. Therefore, the discussion must be approached
with sensitivity to the needs of both sides rather than
focusing only on each party's legal entitlements.

And don't think of mediation as a one-time event. Many
people find it to be a valuable tool for resolving issues at
any point during the divorce process. Use it whenever
you think it might work.

Kids and Money

If the mediation is to be only regarding a specific issue,
then it makes sense to select a mediator that has a strong
background in that area. For example, when mediating
the distribution of business assets it's best to find a
mediator who understands financial reports. A few
hours of training may not be enough. On the other
hand, when it comes to children, mediators who read
complicated business documents as easily as we read
the Brattleboro Reformer might not have much experience in settlements relating to kids.

A dilemma can arise when a couple wants to mediate
their entire divorce settlement. One solution is to use
different mediators for each major issue. Another
approach is to use a single mediator supplemented by
information from lawyers, CPA's, etc.

Keep in mind that the mediator's primary skill is that of
a resolution facilitator. He or she is not expected to
know all the fine points of the law or business or human
psychology, though they should have training in these
areas. Outside experts can be employed to provide the

technical facts. The mediator will then assist the couple in using this information to reach a final settlement.

No matter what number of mediators is utilized (in most cases it will be just one), it's important to separate the discussion of the children from the financial issues. Failure to do this can sometimes result in bargaining the kids against the money. Mediators will make every effort to prevent this from happening. However, creating procedural firewalls is also helpful. For example, agree not to have any discussions on the financial issues until everything about the children is resolved.

Picking the Right Mediator

In Vermont, as in most of the U.S., mediators are largely unregulated. There is no state certification or direct control. Anyone can print a business card declaring that he or she is a mediator. However, this doesn't mean that you can't find excellent mediators in the Green Mountain State.

To Begin with, Woodbury College in Montpelier offers a year long mediation/conflict management training program that has received national recognition. It also conducts shorter three day training sessions for individuals who want to refine their skills.

And the Family Court contracts with a large number of mediators who wish to participate in Vermont's subsidized mediation program for low income households (discussed later in this chapter). Mediators approved by the Family Court must have a total of 100 hours of training in basic and advanced mediation skills, the psychology of divorcing families, domestic and substance abuse, divorce law, and the financial issues related to divorce.

Mediators qualified by the Family Court, in addition, will have 40 hours or more of face-to-face mediation experience. Of this total, 30 hours must involve at least 3 separate divorces including a minimum of direct case supervision/consultation for 5 of those hours.

Keep in mind that all mediators contracted by the Family Court also conduct non-subsidized mediations. So even if you don't qualify for a subsidy the Family Court is a great place to find an experienced mediator.

Many Family Court mediators also belong to the Vermont Mediation Association (VMA). While not all members of the VMA mediate divorces, those that do must have met standards of training and experience similar to the requirements established by the Family Court.

Consider Family Court certification and/or membership in the VMA to be a minimum qualification for any mediator you select. More information and a list of approved mediators can be obtained by visiting any Family Court, by calling toll free 800-622-6359, or by going to the web sites of either the Family Court
                (vermontjudiciary.org)
or the VMA   (http:vma.freeyellow.com).

Another important selection issue is deciding on the style of mediation that will work best for you.

Many mediators feel it's important that the couple develop a settlement on their own. They believe this approach achieves the strongest feeling of "ownership" in the final decision. When the answer comes from the parties themselves and not an outsider, long term success is far more likely. Using this method the mediator helps guide the couple into discovering what works best for them while never making specific recommendations.

But, some mediators see it differently. They reason that many individuals have little or no experience in solving the problems of divorce. Suggesting alternatives that have worked in other cases is not forcing the couple to accept a solution. Their feeling is that without this assistance the solution developed by the parties may be faulty and not lasting. Or that a settlement will never be reached.

Regardless of the philosophy, the key to a successful mediation is that the mediator remains entirely impartial. Other than that, there can be more than one correct approach. What works best in your situation is a matter of personal preference. Get recommendations and interview several mediators. Select the one you and your spouse like best.

Saving Money in Divorce Is a Relative Concept

One benefit of mediation is that mediators are often cheaper than lawyers. And there only has to be one mediator.

The cost of hiring a mediator normally runs from $100 to $200 an hour. The lower amount is more common in rural areas, with the highest often experienced in Burlington and similar locations.

Many mediations are conducted under the Vermont Family Court Mediation Program. In such cases, if both parties are income eligible, the mediator's fee is currently capped at $80 an hour. State subsidies for low income parties can further reduce this amount on a sliding scale

to as little as $10 an hour for up to ten hours of media-
tion. Under some circumstances the ten hour limit can
be exceeded.

If only one spouse's income is low enough to qualify for
the $80 cap, then the higher earning party will pay 50%
of the mediator's normal fee while the other side pays
50% of the reduced amount for which he or she quali-
fies.

The Family Court Mediation Program staff are happy to
provide details on the program including the formula
used to determine income eligibility (see contact information above in this chapter and in the Appendix).

But it isn't only about money. Many people discover
that a better, more satisfying settlement is achieved
through mediation compared to the confrontational
processes of lawyers' letters flying back and forth or
fighting it out in court. Divorce agreements, especially
those involving children, are frequently operational for
many years. Success is far more likely in the long haul
when they are arrived at with the least amount of
"bloodshed."

"Peace in Our Time"

However, feeling good about an agreement is not
always the best measurement. In the late 1930's the
Prime Minister of England sat down with Hitler and
worked out a peace keeping treaty. While he tri-
umphantly returned to London claiming success, the
cataclysmic events of World War II soon proved otherwise. In a somewhat exaggerated fashion this demon-
strates a potential pitfall of the mediation process.

The fact that the parties think they've arrived at a good
deal doesn't automatically mean that the best conclu-

sions have been reached. Many of us admit to being terrible at negotiating the price of a new automobile. So how do we suddenly gain the wisdom to properly represent ourselves in such an emotional and legally complex event as divorce? The short answer is that these skills don't magically improve.

But talented mediators can prevent a catastrophe. While not specifically directing the composition of the settlement the mediator is well aware of what makes sense and what is foolish both legally and logically. If one or both of the parties seem to be going off the deep end the mediator will step in to redirect the effort. Frequently, these problems come up when there is a lack of accurate legal or other specialized information. A single issue may be quickly clarified by having the spouses telephone a lawyer, an accountant, etc. Broader problems may require that these specialists actually attend the mediation.

Having experts participate in the relevant mediation sessions certainly adds some expense, but the alternatives are often less desirable. The lack of critical information on a timely basis can bring a promising discussion to an abrupt halt. Even worse, decisions may be reached that are based on incorrect legal or financial assumptions. Once the error is uncovered, it's really hard to go back and mediate the issue all over again.

Pro se couples might have no choice but to consult a lawyer or other professional on certain topics. The risk of making a serious mistake is just too great.

A perfect example is the West Newbury mother who was prepared to give everything to her husband (including the house, her share of his pension and the vacation home) just so he would grant her custody of the children. The mediator encouraged the woman to consult a lawyer before finalizing the deal and he pointed out that, in her case, she would get the kids regardless of how the assets were divided.

This mother was not happy to give away a property share that was rightfully hers, but acting out of fear and a serious lack of legal knowledge she saw no other choice. The result would have been a financial catastrophe had she not been encouraged to gain expert advice.

Getting It All on Paper

No mediation is legally binding unless both sides agree. But if the goal isn't to reach a joint commitment then it's all just a waste of time. So, hopefully at some point in the mediation a verbal understanding gets put into a document called a memorandum of understanding.

Frequently, these memorandums are signed by the parties, but not always. It depends on what's being resolved and how the agreement will be used. If the mediation deals with issues to be stipulated in Family Court documents (stipulations are discussed in the chapter on Vermont's legal process) it's really not necessary to create a contract during the mediation itself. Later the stipulation will be signed and that's certainly a legal commitment.

On the other hand, if the mediation is to create a separation agreement then that's a different story. Separation agreements are used when the couple is living apart and the court has not yet issued a temporary order. Spouses may operate under a separation agreement for years without ever filing for divorce. If it's important that each side live up to the understanding then it needs to be a signed commitment.

Another good reason to sign all mediation documents is a very practical one. Often when verbal agreements are put into a memorandum for signature one or both of the parties will suddenly get cold feet. If they are still miles apart it's better to find out sooner than later.

Vermonter, Robert Frost??

An important goal in mediation is to break down the adversarial barriers and create an atmosphere of under-standing and trust. That's certainly an effective way to achieve a good resolution. However, once the mediation is over everyone steps back into the hostile "real world."

Legal commitments resulting from mediation are seri-ous business. So it's important to have a lawyer review the understanding to insure it meets current standards for fairness and legality, and to draft any agreement that is going to be signed. It may seem like a waste of money to translate a clear commitment between you and your spouse into complicated legal language. But should it become necessary to enforce the contract in court, that procedure will be quicker, less expensive and the out-come more certain if it was written by a lawyer. Besides, people usually live up to a well drafted agreement that allows little room for interpretation.

To paraphrase a famous Vermonter, Robert Frost, "good agreements make good divorces."

Lots of Ways to Skin a Deer

In the end, a blend of methods works best when negoti-ating with your spouse. Start by sitting down one on one and discussing the situation. Do it in a pleasant, neutral location where you will not be interrupted, preferably not at your house, or your in-law's house.

This is the cheapest and often easiest approach. If help is needed try mediation. Mediation isn't magic, but simply an effective process for putting people in a position to reach a common understanding. It's still up to the divorcing spouses to find that understanding.

Keep your attorney informed if you have one. Pro se couples shouldn't be afraid to consult a lawyer occasionally as well. And stay open minded to all settlement options. Sometimes giving in on something of less value to you than to your partner will deliver back an item you really treasure. Remember, compromise is not a sign of weakness, it is evidence of intelligence.

CHAPTER 5

Parental Rights and Responsibilities and Parent-Child Contact

No Kid Jokes, but Some Definitions

In Vermont the rights of children are taken very seriously. So try directing those tongue and cheek comments about divorce at other, more inviting, targets like your mother-in-law or your spouse's new boyfriend.

Knowing that not everyone will take such a benevolent attitude, Vermont's legal process keeps the children issues as far away from the rest of the divorce proceedings as possible. This cuts down the chances to use children as bargaining chips, especially with respect to property distribution.

Before jumping into details, let's go over two definitions. The first involves what used to fall under the term child custody. Nowadays it's called parental rights and responsibilities (P R & R). The other deals with visitation rights and is currently referred to as parent-child contact (P-C C). This book uses the old and new terms interchangeably.

P R & R — the rights and responsibilities related to a child's physical living arrangements, parent-child contact, education, medical and dental care, religion, travel and any other matter involving a child's welfare and upbringing.

P-C C — the right of a parent who does not have physical responsibility (the parent not having physical custody of the child) to have visitation with the child.

While some lawyers and mediators may dislike using out of date words like custody and visitation it does serve a purpose. Many people still use these words all the time as do some law books. Including them here makes the material easier to follow and understand. By the end of this chapter everyone will he comfortable with P R & R and P-C C as well.

What Custody Really Means

Knowing that P R & R is like custody and P-C C is like visitation really doesn't tell you everything. In fact, these terms can be misleading. Many people think that custody is only about which parent will live with the kids. Actually, the term refers to both legal and physical control over the children. These are separate issues and full of additional sub-control possibilities. Custody awards are often not a single decision, but a collection of assigned rights and responsibilities involving both parents.

Legal custody (often called legal responsibility) has to do with parents making decisions on schooling, medical care, religion, and other welfare issues. What kind of school the children go to (anyone for home schooling?), what sports team they can play on (football is too dangerous!), what dentist is used (do you believe in holistic healing?), etc. are some of the decisions that a parent who has sole legal custody gets to make.

Physical custody (frequently called physical responsibility or simply "custody") deals mostly with the power to determine the location of a child's primary residence. In broad terms, the parent with sole physical responsibility decides if the child will reside in South Burlington, South Dorset, South Carolina or South America. He or she can even decide that the child should live with someone else, such as a grandparent.

That's because Vermont law gives a lot of flexibility to the parent having sole physical custody. However, this power is not absolute and can be subject to legal review (see below).

It sometimes boils down to each parent gaining sole responsibility for some elements of their children's custody. One may get sole legal custody for all kid issues except religion and healthcare, while the other parent receives sole legal responsibility for those two items. In addition, one of the parents gets sole physical custody and the other just visitation rights. Think of the unlimited possibilities for dividing things up.

As you can see, custody is about more than just who gets the kids. The term parental rights and responsibilities (P R & R) really does do a better job of describing what is involved.

A Note on Moving the Kids

The parent with physical custody has significant authority, but it's not always a blank check to move the children from here to Timbuktu. Let's assume the non-custodial parent has a strong relationship with the kids and gets a lot of P-C C (visitation) under the final order. The court may listen to a complaint stating that relocating the children to a distant area violates the non-custodial parent's P-C C rights. This argument can be strengthened if the child has other important reasons to remain in the local area, or at least the U.S. (loving grandparents, special school, ace pitcher for a championship baseball team, etc.).

Let's just say that the power a parent with physical custody has to move the kids is not a total certainty. It's possible that making a big move could reopen the entire custody issue based on what is best for the children, especially if there are other factors involved, such as questions regarding the quality of the custodial parent's care. Therefore, consulting a lawyer before making a dramatic change in location is strongly advised.

If your spouse receives sole physical custody, try to persuade him or her to give you a vote on major relocations. The judge cannot force the custodial spouse to do this. It's up to your out-of-court negotiating skills to obtain such a right (you might have to give up something to get something). Should you make the deal, be sure it gets written into the final divorce order.

Not an All or Nothing Game

So far we've been talking in terms of sole P R & R awards only, but it doesn't have to be an all or nothing game. Instead of giving sole responsibility to one parent, the court can make one or more of the items a shared responsibility (also called joint custody). Under joint custody each parent has a 50% vote.

Shared physical custody means the parents must reach agreement on where the kid's primary residence will be now and in the future. The same can be done with legal custody. Parents might share responsibility on all the legal issues (healthcare, education, religion, etc.) or it could be sole responsibility on some and shared on others.

But, before you jump on the joint custody bandwagon make sure you and your spouse are up to task. If every "consultation" is going to be like World War II, think of the effect it will have on the children not to mention each other.

That's why the court never grants shared responsibility unless both parents agree to it. If either side raises an objection then the judge will simply grant sole authority to one parent (or each parent might end up with sole responsibility for different custody issues).

Even if both parents willingly seek a shared arrangement it can run off the tracks now and again. That's why all shared custody agreements include a dispute resolution provision (such as requiring mediation) to reconcile these differences.

Splitting the Babies

There is still one more way things might go. The judge can award sole custody of some of the children to one parent and sole custody of the rest to the second parent. This is called split custody and it can be used for setting out physical responsibilities (which child lives primarily with which parent).

Now, the court is even more cautious about granting split custody than it is when granting joint custody. Separating brothers and sisters into two different households is not high on any judge's agenda and is rarely done. However, split custody will be authorized if that's what both parents want and the situation looks like it makes sense for the kids. After all, there is something to be said for youngsters being managed by a same sex parent as they become "teeny boppers."

Unlike in the case of shared custody, the court will sometimes order split custody even if only one parent requests it and the judge feels it's in the best interest of the children. That's because split physical responsibility does not require the parents to agree on anything in the future. Each side has sole physical custody for some of the children. There is no joint decision making.

Let's face it, the judge is often between a rock and a hard place when it comes to dividing up custody. Judgments are tough to make and sometimes have less than perfect results. It's no fun taking away a parent's right to manage his or her children. At the same time, it's definitely not in the best interests of the kids for the parties to go for each other's throat every time a decision has to be made.

Some Confusion in Custody Orders

Just because one parent gets sole physical responsibility doesn't mean the youngsters only stay with that parent. Normally, a child spends at least 50% of the time with the parent having sole physical responsibility. That means that a parent having no physical custody rights might also have the child for up to half the time. Whatever the judge's decision, it gets nicely laid out in the parent-child contact order.

Looking at legal custody, you may find the opposite situation. Remember that if legal responsibilities are shared (joint) then the child welfare decisions are a 50-50 affair. However, it's possible for one of the parents having joint legal custody (a 50% vote on welfare issues) to see the child only a few weeks a year. Maybe he or she lives in California or travels all the time. It can be confusing.

Getting to Know the Players

Okay, now that the terminology has been explained, here's how the process works. You'll meet two key players while venturing into Vermont's legal maze of P R & R, P-C C and child support: the Family Court judge and the Family Court magistrate.

Initially, the Family Court judge determines the temporary order for custodial responsibilities and parent-child contact. Later on the judge will issue the final P R & R and P-C C orders. In both cases, this may be as simple as approving an agreement submitted by the parties or it can be left totally up to the court to decide.

Originally, the Family Court magistrate's only job was setting the amount of child support each parent must pay. However, as the Family Court becomes increasingly backlogged, magistrates are frequently called upon to approve temporary custody and P-C C arrangements stipulated by the parents (read about stipulations below). Generally, only the judge and not the magistrate will issue temporary P R & R and P-C C orders when none have been stipulated by the parents.

The CMSC and Temporary Hearings

Shortly after filing the complaint, the spouses will meet in the offices of the Family Court (along with attorneys if they are being used) for the case manager's status conference (CMSC). The CMSC was previously discussed in the chapter describing Vermont's overall divorce process. So, let's just focus here on P R & R and P-C C.

Along with other duties, the clerk at the CMSC will collect all agreements the parties have reached regarding custody and visitation (these agreements are called stipulations or "stips" for short). The stips related to P R & R and P-C C are then forwarded to the judge (sometimes to the magistrate to spread out the work) for review and approval. The court doesn't automatically accept stips just because the parents have agreed to them. But, the judge or magistrate usually will go along with reasonable proposals.

If the parents fail to come up with agreements on P R & R and/or P-C C by the end of the CMSC, a temporary hearing will be scheduled with the Family Court judge within 30 days of the filing date, but sooner if there is an emergency. The first thing that must be decided at this hearing is temporary custody and visitation, as nothing else can be done until these two issues are resolved. Whether the parties work out a deal themselves or the court imposes its decision, the results become part of the temporary order.

Don't be misled by the term "temporary" when applied to the custody and visitation orders. These decisions create a framework for the final order that can be difficult to change once in place. For example, a temporary order that grants a spouse who is clearly the primary caregiver sole physical and legal custody is likely to be made permanent in the final order. Remember, shared custody cannot be imposed by the court unless both parties agree. Visitation is not so rigidly carried over to the final order, but the longer a temporary arrangement goes on the harder it is to change. Because the stakes are high, lawyers will often "pull out all the stops" at the temporary hearing.

Yet, it is also an opportunity for the two sides to try a more cooperative approach. The temporary hearing occurs only 30 days after the divorce filing and tempers can be hot. This may not be the best environment to make lasting decisions regarding such emotional children issues. Assuming no serious problems exist with either of the parents (drugs, abuse, etc.) much can be gained by trying a shared custody arrangement with visitation that recognizes the importance of the kids in both spouses' lives. The judge will appreciate the effort the parties are making and remain flexible as to the final custody/visitation structure.

If the parents have good intentions, nothing is lost during this trial period of cooperation. Frequently, by the final hearing they will have arrived at a mutually agreeable arrangement. If not, the battle that would have taken place at the temporary hearing just gets relocated to the final hearing.

Once child custody/visitation is settled the matter of child support goes before the magistrate at a separate hearing. This is also supposed to be done within 30 days of the filing date, but after P R & R and P-C C is determined (see more on this in the child support chapter).

A Do It Yourself Guide

As mentioned earlier in this chapter, there is an easier way to settle parental rights and responsibilities (custody) issues. A smart couple will figure out something on their own. After all, who can be certain what the court will decide? A parent unwilling to compromise with the reasonable requests of the other party may end up with no rights at all. It happens all the time!

Assuming the parents have the good sense to put together their own agreement (using professional help as needed), sole, joint and split custody responsibilities can be mixed and matched as desired. They just need to make sure that all the important issues are covered. These include at least the following seven items:

1. Physical living arrangements

2. Parent-child contact

3. Education of the minor children

4. Medical, dental and heath care issues

5. Travel arrangements for visitation

6. Procedures for the parents to communicate about the children's welfare issues

7. Procedures for making decisions on future shared responsibility issues when the parents can't reach agreement on their own (arbitration, mediation, etc.)

In Vermont, any agreement between the parents that divides or shares P R & R is presumed by the court to be in the best interest of the children. That means the judge will almost always agree to what the parents propose.

The Nine Magic Questions

However, if the parties are determined to disagree the court will not hesitate to step in. In Vermont nine items are considered when deciding who gets the kids and other P R & R issues.

1. The kind of relationship that the child has with each parent and how well each parent gives love, affection, and guidance to the child.

This is about the quality of each parent's relationship with their children. Most parents love their children very much, but not all do. Most parents nurture and guide their children properly, but some don't do as good a job as others. Obviously, the court wants to fully understand the answer to this question.

2. The effort that each parent makes to assure that the child receives adequate food, clothing, medical care, and other material needs and a safe environment.

We are not necessarily talking about starving the kids to death. But the court will not be pleased if one party's idea of having a good time is a daily diet limited to fast food burgers and taking five year olds on November hunting trips to Harmonyville.

3. How well each parent insures that the current and future development needs of the child are met.

Do you help the children with their homework, go to PTA meetings, support their participation in scouting, music lessons or one of a million other possibilities? Does your spouse? Who does it best? Keep in mind this is more than just attending meetings and teaching a kid how to fish. The activities have to relate to what is appropriate for each stage of the child's development.

4. How well the child is adjusted to the child's present living conditions (housing, school, and community) and the effect that any change would have on the child.

If giving custody to one of the parties means that the children will have to start a new life many miles away or maybe across the country, that is a major change. How will it affect the star goalie when he has to leave the local hockey team? The same goes for trading a home and favorite horse in Island Pond for condo life and a goldfish in the New Jersey suburbs.

> 5. *How well each parent is able to foster in the child a positive relationship with the other parent, including physical contact (unless such contact would be harmful to the child).*

The court has no interest in giving responsibility to someone that attempts to destroy the child's relationship with the other parent.

> 6. *The quality of the child's relationship with the primary caregiver taking into account the child's age and development.*

Like Fred Sanford used to say on TV, "This is the big one!" Fred was talking about his heart and question six truly gets to the heart of the decision making process. If you are the primary caregiver and have a great parent-child relationship you are 75% of the way to getting the kids. The term "primary caregiver" is explained below.

> 7. *The relationship of the child with persons (other than the parents) who may significantly affect the child.*

If granting physical custody to one parent will likely result in the loss of positive outside relationships, due to relocation or other reasons, the court will give that consideration. This often involves losing contact with the grandparents, but it can also be about other adults who are important in the child's life. It certainly includes the impact of leaving close friends and schoolmates.

8. *How well the parents communicate and cooperate with each other and make joint decisions about the child if the parental rights are to be shared.*

If the court is being asked to issue shared custody rights then there must be some reason to believe that the two parents can work reasonably well together when it comes to dealing with the kids.

9. *Finally, the court will take into account any evidence of abuse and the impact of the abuse on the relationship between the child and the abusing parent.*

If there is a history of spousal abuse (particularly if it's done in front of the kids) the court will want to limit the exposure of the children to such events. Of course, if child abuse is the issue then the decision is obvious.

Making a Run for the Roses

Generally, it doesn't take a rocket scientist to answer the above nine questions. The fact is that both parents usually love their kids, want the best for them, and give them as much attention as possible. But in most families parenting chores are not equally shared due to a combination of reasons. This makes the spouse doing most of the caregiving (the primary caregiver) easy to spot and more often than not he or she gets physical responsibility and his or her home becomes the primary residence.

For many years the mom was virtually always given physical custody. Lately, that has changed somewhat, but not as much as you may think. Mothers still win custody most of the time because they are usually the main caregiver and not just because they are the mom. So, if you have not been doing the majority of the parenting, but desperately want the kids, some big changes have to be made.

Twelve months before even filing for divorce start acting like the primary caregiver of the children. Make all the parent-teacher conferences, drive the kids to the doctor and dentist, stay home when they are sick, do their laundry and their shopping, attend the school concerts and all their other activities, put them to bed, bathe them, cook for them, comfort and discipline them, etc. In other words be the ideal parent.

Having done all that, you may find that your spouse (who was doing most of the caregiving up to this point) will forget any idea of divorce, since you've turned yourself into such great partner! Many divorces are simply about people taking each other and their family for granted.

Assuming that doesn't happen and you really feel there is a chance to get the kids, DO NOT move out of the house. Leaving the children with your spouse before the temporary order is issued tells the court who you think is the primary caregiver. The only exception would be if you are an abused spouse and it isn't safe to remain at home (better to get out and find a lawyer immediately).

Keep in mind the difficulty of altering the court's P R & R decisions. Look at it this way. The P R & R is carved in slow drying cement. The longer it's in place the harder it is to change. Yes, it might be fine tuned later on, but not without significant effort and a substantial change in circumstances of one or both of the parties having occurred. So if you plan to challenge the ruling there better be a really good reason that brings into question the other parent's character or capability (drug use, abuse, etc.) with witnesses to prove it.

One last thought. It's not unusual during the marriage for the wife to be the primary caregiver of one kid, while the husband is the primary caregiver of a second. While a split custody order is possible, the court doesn't like to do that. Most likely, one parent will get physical custody of all the youngsters. Being a judge is not as easy as it looks.

How to Mess Things Up

Some parents overplay their hand when going for P R & R.

A woman from Proctorsville was determined to get sole physical and legal custody of her child. Actually, there was no doubt that the kid would be staying with her, but the husband wanted to share the P R & R. In order to prevent this from happening she accused the husband of molesting the child. Even though the father proved he was innocent, it became difficult for him to touch his daughter for fear of his actions being misinterpreted.

Making this kind of false accusation can result in the judge awarding the children to the injured party even when the accusing parent would normally have received physical custody. There is simply no justification for using such deceptive tactics.

In another case, an East Wallingford couple was involved in a very hostile divorce. The mother was the primary caregiver and the husband used his visitation time to turn his son against the mother. Eventually the boy refused to return home. This resulted in significant legal wrangling. Finally, the judge came up with a solution. For every day the boy did not spend at his mother's house (except as allowed by the P-C C), the father was fined $100. In short order, the boy was sleeping at home once more.

In difficult divorces like the ones above, it's important to keep a diary covering your spouse, kids, and the divorce in general. Make it simple. Purchase a large calendar and write the daily events in the boxes provided for each day. The divorce process may take a year or more and it's hard to remember exactly when each thing happened or how often.

Now a Word to the Wise

Even if you know that the court will give you the kids and decide most issues in your favor, try to work things out with your spouse rather than relying on the legal system. While many aspects of a divorce are a one time deal, raising the children, whether the parents are married or divorced, is a long term joint project. A court imposed decision that you love and your spouse hates will come back to haunt you. It doesn't take any great intelligence to realize that the parents, assuming good intentions on both sides, will be able to work out a better plan than the court. If you need some help, try using mediation.

Keep your attorney updated on the negotiation process. This will allow you to stay informed of the rights and obligations both parents have under the law. And make sure a lawyer reviews all agreements before you sign them.   Once they're signed it's difficult to go back requesting changes because you didn't understand the deal or you forgot to include an item.

The Court Can Help

Another option for spouses struggling to agree on P-C C (so called high conflict cases) is the Parent Coordination Program and it's a good one.   This program is administered by the Family Court and combines an investigation with a kind of mediation. At the parties' request the judge will select a parent coordinator to perform this service from a list of qualified individuals (an experienced mediator, school principal, etc.).

The coordinator contacts the two parties in person or by telephone to review their concerns (the parents may or may not meet together). If the children are old enough they will also be interviewed. Through this process an attempt is made to resolve the outstanding problems regarding the children. However, if no agreement is reached then the parent coordinator sends his or her recommendations to the Family Court. A hearing to review these recommendations is held and the judge eventually issues an order deciding the matter.

The Parent Coordination Program started in 2002 and can be utilized before or after the divorce to work out issues related to parent-child contact. The fee of around $80 an hour is spilt between the parents. Charges are reduced based on the parent's ability to pay.

A Call to Arms!

Unfortunately, not everyone is willing to put the good of their children above their own self-interest. There is nothing meaner in the entire divorce process than an all-out custody/visitation battle. In its worst form this is not merely a nasty litigation, it's a nuclear war, a jihad, a total suspension of reason and decency. Like Godzilla meeting a junkyard dog.

While not often used, either spouse can request, and sometimes the court on its own will demand, that a forensic evaluation be undertaken. A psychologist is called in to methodically interview the parents and children along with friends, neighbors, school counselors, any therapists working with the kids, etc. In addition, each family member takes a written psychological test.

Youngsters too small to do a written test are given an oral one.

The study requires 4 to 8 weeks to complete and costs between $3,000 and $7,500. Normally, the parties share the expense. In the end, the approximately 30 page report boils down everything into recommendations on both P R & R and P-C C.

But even without a forensic evaluation both lawyers will be working overtime preparing for the trial. A parade of expert witnesses may have to be called in as well. Every skeleton in every closet is dragged out for probing and display. You will recall that divorce trials are open to the public along with most of the court documents. Think about that.

All this is expensive. A first class custody/visitation battle can run $50,000 per side or more. Remember, that doesn't include the other divorce issues. It's not surprising that such warfare tends to increase in proportion to the client's ability to pay. Often, if they really have a lot of money then they mostly fight over the money and leave the kid issues alone. Greed has its virtues.

Kids Don't Vote and Rarely Testify

Some parents believe that the kids get a vote when deciding P R & R and P-C C. Maybe this idea comes from the movies, TV dramas, or whatever, but the answer in Vermont is "No they don't." Until a child is 18 years old (or emancipated) the parents, the custodial parent, a guardian, or the court makes those decisions.

Children are usually not even allowed to testify in a custody/visitation trial. Most kids want to stay with both parents and the court feels it's psychologically damaging to force them to choose one over the other.

Nevertheless, under special circumstances, a child will testify in order to establish certain facts in the case. It's only done when there is no other witness that can be used. The judge must be convinced that the value of the testimony outweighs the possible harm to the child.

This is no small matter for the court. The judge will appoint a separate lawyer to represent the rights of the youngster who will testify. In addition, a "guardian ad litem" is assigned. The guardian ad litem is neither a lawyer nor a social worker. He or she is an adult volunteer without legal training who is there to buffer the child from aggressive parents, lawyers and the system in general.

By now you realize that nothing under the law is absolute. So, it's no surprise that older kids (around 15 years and up) sometimes have a way of getting their desires, either directly or indirectly, known to the court. How much influence do they have? All things being equal, a judge would like to please them. However, the court recognizes that teens, as well as younger kids, don't always have a complete understanding of the situation.

Vermont, Love It or Leave It

Everything in this chapter is based on the divorce taking place in Vermont. But what happens if the children have been moved or are scheduled to move out of the state?

In virtually all cases the Family Court judge will issue an interim order as soon as the divorce complaint is filed. This interim order prohibits either party from moving out of state with the children unless the court gives its approval or the written consent of the other parent is obtained. Any unapproved move is a violation of the order.

However, it's a different situation prior to the divorce filing. Vermont law provides both parents with equal rights to the kids and so either party can do what he or she wishes as long as there is no court order stating otherwise. But does anyone want the children to get caught up in a tug of war across state lines?

Putting aside this emotional aspect, moving out of Vermont prior to a divorce filing can put in question where the divorce should take place. Courts, not only the ones in Vermont, don't like a "forum shopper" (a parent that moves to another state in order to get under a friendlier jurisdiction). Judges will also give the relocating spouse a hard time if the move was made to make it difficult for the other parent to see the kids.

This doesn't mean that it's impossible to move from Vermont. Just make sure it's for a good reason, such as the mom who can't afford to stay in the marriage home and so she moves in with her out of state parents. Or one of the parties may need the emotional support of distant family members and friends.

Maybe it's just too darn cold. Divorce is often brought on by the harsh Vermont winters, especially if one spouse is from the South. Just ask the real estate agents that sell and resell the same houses on Isle La Motte to newlyweds having one spouse from out of state.

So use your head. If you must head off to the tropics, or anywhere else, try to work out a deal with your spouse before going. If you can't reach agreement and there is a legitimate reason to relocate then seek a court ruling in advance of the move.

In the end, the state where the youngsters have the most contacts is the state where the children issues will be decided. That's where all the witnesses able to describe the needs of the children and the relationship of the children with their parents can be found.

If the kids have not lived in a state for at least six months that state will rarely hear the case. However, if a spouse and the kids have lived outside of Vermont for a long enough period then there is a good chance that the divorce can be handled in the new state. In that situation, you'll need to buy a different book!

Things to Consider about Visitation

The first thing parents want to know is how the court will decide custody. While they are interested in legal responsibility, their greatest concerns are what will be the children's primary residence and what P-C C (visitation) rights are likely to be granted. You should have a good idea on how the primary residence is decided, but what about visitation? Remember, it's possible for a child to be ordered to spend up to 50% of the time with the non-custodial parent.

There is no easy way to predict visitation rulings since many issues enter into the formula. Naturally, the distance the two parents live from each other represents a practical limitation. It can be just too time consuming and expensive to shuttle the children back and forth across great distances every month, no less every weekend.

Anyway, kids need to attend one school all year, stay in touch with their friends and keep up with extra-curricular activities. So, if the non-custodial parent is beyond school commuting distance then overnights during the week are probably out.

The age of the children also matters. Not so long ago psychologists were saying that toddlers must not have overnights with the non-custodial parent. It was felt that little kids needed the stability gained by staying in a single home environment all the time. Frequent (even daily) visits from the non-custodial parent were encouraged, but they had to occur at the primary residence.

Apparently those doctors ignored all the little ones being shuttled back and forth to daycare centers and grandparents' homes with no ill effects while the spouses worked. Nowadays, the court often permits toddlers to overnight part of each week at the non-custodial parent's home.

Clearly both parents have to understand the basics of child development no matter what the situation. Get a book on the subject and share it with your spouse. It's a great way to reduce the arguments over a visitation schedule. The bottom line is that kids are pretty tough and can get used to a lot of shifting around when parents make an effort to deal with all the uncertainties and concerns that children naturally develop.

If This Is Wells River It Must Be Tuesday

This section attempts to summarize the kind of visitation arrangements judges have been known to make. Of course the assumption is that both parents are acceptable to the court and both want the children as much as is possible. Remember that the only thing that is certain in divorce is the uncertainty. Please don't ask for your money back on the book if you end up with something different. Experts who advise the court are constantly revising their thoughts on what is the right thing to do. And judges have a great amount of discretion in these matters, so court orders can vary quite a bit.

To keep things simple the possibilities are divided up based on the age of the children and whether the non-custodial parent is near or far way. How far is far away? Well if the children cannot attend their regular school when visiting the non-custodial parent then that parent is far away. However, there's a big difference between being 60 miles and 600 miles far away. At 60 miles frequent weekend overnights are quite possible, but it would be very difficult at 600 miles. So you have to apply some time and cost logic to these general guidelines.

Infants

Live nearby or far away—A lot has changed regarding infants in the last few years. At one time overnights with the non-custodial father were rarely allowed. "A baby needs to be with its mother" is no longer the golden rule. Today, overnights at the non-custodial parent's home are fairly common. How far away the non-custodial parent lives will affect how often these visits can occur. But the message from the experts now is that children five and under should be "overnighting" with both parents every few days in order to fully bond with them. After the age of five the kids can be away from a parent for longer periods without affecting the relationship.

1 to 5 Years of Age

Live nearby—Overnights can start at once a week and build up to three nights a week. Alternate weekend and holiday overnights as well.

Live far away—Overnight two or three weekends per month and alternate holiday overnights.

6 to 8 Years of Age

Live nearby—Overnights can start at one a week and build up to three a week. After a while overnights can build up to alternating full weeks, alternate weekends and holiday overnights.

Live far away—Overnights two or three weekends per month and alternate holiday overnights. Two-week-long visits during the summer, at Christmas, and school breaks. Towards the upper end of age range (8 years old) four week visits are possible for the summer, or when practical.

9 to 12 Years of Age

Live nearby—Alternate up to two weeks in each residence and alternate holiday overnights. Four to six week stays during the summer.

Live far away—Overnights two or three weekends per month. Alternate holiday overnights. If too far for frequent weekends then overnights on the long weekends (President's Day, Thanksgiving, etc.). Also, half of the Christmas break and all the spring break. Four to six week stays during the summer.

13 to 18 Years of Age

Basically the same as the 9 to 12 years old schedule. The big difference is that you are now dealing with teenagers who often have active lives. While children don't get to "vote" on the visitation schedule, their reasonable desires should be given consideration.

If prom night is on the day a child is to stay with an out of town non-custodial parent the overnight schedule will need to be altered. On the other hand, if a teenager makes a hair styling appointment that conflicts with visitation there is nothing wrong with the parent insisting that the appointment be changed.

The approach to resolving these issues is no different than if the parents were still married. It's not going to be a successful relationship if a parent chooses to ignore things which the children think are important. Just stay flexible.

For a Really Distant Parent

In situations where the "live far away" arrangements shown above result in unreasonable costs and/or travel time requirements, a less frequent and simpler schedule of visits becomes necessary.

For kids up to age four visitation is usually just a week here and there (when practical) and whenever the non-custodial parent is in the area where the child lives. However, once the child reaches five years old a more formal structure can be maintained. This might be along the lines of spending most of the summer with the non-custodial parent, as well as alternate Christmases and either the winter or spring break.

Finally, some parents try to use the child's "preference" to undermine the visitation rights of the other parent. "Would you rather come with me to the big rock and roll concert this weekend or do your overnights with your dad?" Not only is this not permissible, it is very destructive.

It Should Only Be So Simple

You might think that the judge would lay out a visitation program that changes as the children develop. No such luck. If the divorce involves an eight-month-old baby the court will order visitation rights that are appropriate

for that age. Unless the non-custodial parent goes back
to court to get them revised as the child develops the
original visitation rights will still be the same when the
kid is 18 years old.

Assuming the children are very young at the time of the
divorce, it's possible that, over the years, the non-custodial parent will have to go back to court several times
requesting visitation changes. It's sure a lot simpler and
less expensive when both parents just work things out
between themselves. However, to be on the safe side try
to get the judge to include in the final order an automat-
ic review of the visitation schedule when a specific event
occurs (child begins school, reaches five years old, etc.).

CHAPTER 6

Child Support

Don't Wait to Be Asked

Things are often in motion before the divorce filing takes place. Frequently one spouse has moved out of the house, while the other spouse stays at home with the kids and becomes the de facto custodial parent (at least on a temporary basis). It's also pretty clear what the children's needs are and the amount of money each parent is able to pay. So why should the non-custodial parent wait for the court to issue a child support order? The kids need the money now.

Making voluntary child support payments before the judge orders them (even ahead of the divorce filing) is just smart thinking. It reduces the pressure on the custodial parent who is facing the physical and financial demands of raising the family alone. Also, it gives everyone a chance to catch their breath while getting emotions under control. Sometimes, in this improved environment, the divorce filing can be delayed and an attempt made to reconcile the marriage. The same logic applies to voluntary spousal support payments (alimony) as well.

But if there's no money coming in to pay for the children's expenses, you can be sure that the acting custodial parent will be rushing to court to secure child support (most likely by filing for divorce). And it won't take long to get it. Vermont law requires that a child support order (the amount each spouse pays to support the children) must be issued within 30 days of the divorce filing date. In reality, it takes a little longer because the P R & R and P-C C have to be decided first and the system is often overworked. However, everything is usually in place within 60 to 90 days.

The reluctant to pay non-custodial parent gains little by postponing the inevitable. That's because child support orders are usually retroactive (calculated from the day of the divorce filing) unless the magistrate feels that payments already made by the non-custodial spouse since the filing date were sufficient. Yet, delays often arise when the custodial parent asks for too much money or one spouse is trying to punish the other, or the non-custodial parent is acting foolish.

Making Everybody Happy

A written agreement isn't required in order to make voluntary payments. However, putting the plan in writing clarifies what each side expects of the other. This tends to have a calming effect. Often the payment structure is included in an overall separation agreement (read about separation agreements in the chapter on the divorce process).

At the time of the Case Manager's Status Conference (the CMSC is described in the chapter on the divorce process) the details of any voluntary child support payments are usually submitted to the court clerk. The clerk then sends these stipulations to the magistrate for review and approval. Normally, the prefiling support payments are maintained until the magistrate issues the child support order.

If the parties at the CMSC wish to change the pre-filing child support payments that revised amount is put in the stipulation. Should the parents fail to agree on the change then the magistrate will decide the amount at the initial child support hearing. Again, things continue as before until that time.

Here's a tip. Making generous pre-filing child support payments is usually rewarded. The magistrate will not feel that the pre-filing support amount is an indication of what temporary or permanent payments should be assigned. The court understands that in the early days of a separation there is usually a greater need for money then over the longer term. Meanwhile, the magistrate is left thinking that the non-custodial parent is a great guy or gal.

The reverse is also true. A magistrate is likely to go harder on a non-custodial parent who is trying to avoid or delay contributing a fare share to the needs of the kids when clearly he or she is able to provide the money.

Let's Meet the OCS

The Office of Child Support (OCS) helps administer the Child Support Guidelines. These are the tables the magistrate uses to figure out each parent's child support responsibility (different tables are used depending on how P-C C is divided). As explained in the chapter on Vermont's divorce process, the guidelines were developed in order to get more uniform judgments while insuring that the minimum needs of the children are met.

The OCS also represents the interests of the state in collecting child support when the custodial parent is on
welfare or when the child is in state custody. That's
because a person on welfare must turn over any child
support received to Vermont. Of course, if the child support exceeds the welfare payments the state only gets to
keep an amount equal to the welfare amount. Usually
the support payments are less than the welfare figure.

Finally, the most visible function of the OCS is when it is
assisting the custodial parent (never the non-custodial
parent) on child support issues. This includes going
before the magistrate at the child support hearing where
the initial support payment is being determined, as well
as later on when adjustments to the order are requested.

The OCS charges nothing for this service. Despite the
"freebie" some people prefer to have their attorney do
this work alone or together with the OCS. Discuss the
options with your lawyer and decide what makes sense
for you. Of course, if you have no lawyer using the OCS
is a great idea. (800-786-3241/www.ocs.state.vt.us)

The Child Support Guidelines Categories

Now that you know where the guidelines come from
let's take a look at how they are used. If you are reading
this late at night you may want to hold off until the
morning. It's not the easiest process to follow.

Okay, here we go. You will recall that support payments
cannot be determined until the P R & R and P-C C is settled. This is because the magistrate must know the
schedule for time sharing with the children in order to
select the proper Child Support Guidelines category to
use and how to split the payments between the parents.

Child Support Guidelines Categories:

• **SOLE CUSTODY GUIDELINE**—When one parent has physical custody of a child more than 75% of the calendar year. The child support calculation is based on having to keep only one household for the children. Therefore, a higher child support payment by the non-custodial parent is possible.

• **SHARED CUSTODY GUIDELINE**—When each parent exercises physical custody 30% or more each calendar year. The child support guidelines are adjusted (compared to sole custody guidelines) because now two households have to be maintained for the children. In this case, the child support payment is spread proportionately (based on each parent's income and percentage of custody time), rather than having the entire amount going to one parent as in a sole custody situation. When one parent has physical custody at least 25% but less than 30% of the calendar year there is an adjustment, but not as great.

• **SPLIT CUSTODY GUIDELINE**—When each parent has physical custody of at least one child. In this case, the child support calculation becomes really complicated (especially if there are different numbers of children with each parent and some are sole custody and some are shared).

To come up with the split custody payments the magistrate, using the appropriate guidelines, calculates how much the parents should receive in child support for the children each has in custody. These two amounts are subtracted from each other and the difference is paid to the parent who was entitled to the most child support. So if it works out that the dad should get $500 a month and the mom should get $800 a month the magistrate simply orders the husband to pay the wife $300 ($800 minus $500). The mom pays nothing to the dad.

You are not alone if all this is still unclear. Don't give up, your lawyer or accountant or the OCS will be able to get pretty close to the figure that you will probably pay or receive.

Amusing Facts About Custody Percentages

In Vermont, custody percentages are based on the number of overnights per calendar year that a youngster spends with each parent. If the child stays every weekend with mom (two overnights a week) that totals 104 days or 28% of the year (104 divided by 365). Don't forget to include who gets the kids on what holidays. That calculation should be pretty clear.

Now grab your chair and follow this closely. Child support categories do not reflect the P R & R order (custody) even though the identical category names (sole, shared and split custody) are used. Instead, they are based upon the P-C C order (visitation). For example, the family court judge might issue a P R & R order giving you sole physical custody. The P-C C order by the same judge says that your spouse (the non-custodial parent) will have the children every weekend and two weeks in the summer (31% of the year).

In this case the magistrate will use the joint custody category of the Child Support Guidelines (because each parent has the children at least 25% of the time) when figuring out the support payment. The magistrate doesn't care that you are the sole custodial parent (the P R & R order). Under the P-C C your spouse has the kids 31%

of the time and that's what counts. So why do the guidelines use the term "custody" when the calculation is based on "visitation"? Hey, this is your government and it's here to help!

Here's another tricky issue. Usually, the magistrate will base the child support payments strictly on the P R & R and P-C C order. However, there is room to dispute this payment if the non-custodial parent is not actually seeing the child as much as the order provides.

For example, the P-C C order might give each parent the children 50% of the time. But suppose the kids actually spend 90% of their time with one parent (maybe the other parent travels too much). The custodial parent could argue that the magistrate should disregard the P-C C order and use the sole custody guideline. How things get decided depends a lot on the reasons and circumstances surrounding the events. Leeway is usually given for missed overnights due to illness or special events. In high conflict cases it is wise to keep a record of all visits, missed visits, etc.

As you can see, custody percentages are very important when it comes to how much child support each parent pays or receives. Keep that in mind when developing a visitation agreement with your spouse. If it works out so that you will have the youngster overnight 24% of the time or 29% of the time, change it so you have 25% or 30% custody (the minimum percentages that trigger a sharing of the child support amount). However, there are cases where going from sole custody guidelines to joint custody guidelines result in a higher payment. When this happens the judge will almost always use whatever amount is lower. But this decision remains at the discretion of the court.

Calculating Parental Income

It should be obvious that each parent's income is a key factor in determining child support payments. That's because the child support guidelines take into account both the needs of the kids and how much money is available. More surprising may be the fact that Vermont has its own way of calculating how much you earn (or should earn, or could earn). In many cases the income reported to the IRS is merely a starting point.

Since income affects several other divorce issues in addition to child support, a separate chapter has been dedicated to this discussion. However, let's touch on a few of the key items here.

Basically, the court expects that everyone should work. If a parent doesn't work there needs to be a good reason. Usually, the magistrate will accept a custodial parent remaining home with preschool or disabled children. However, if the kids are healthy and school age the assumption is that both parents need to earn a living.

To get this point across the magistrate will evaluate a non-working parent's job skills and then simply assume a certain level of income adjusted for any assumed daycare expenses (called imputed income). Based on this assumption the magistrate will require that a non-working parent pay his or her fair share of child support. The fact that the parent is not working and currently has no income doesn't always matter to the court (it's up to the discretion of the magistrate).

Important Adjustments to Income

Now that the magistrate has figured out each party's income it's time to subtract the allowable deductions. A common income adjustment is the cost of the children's health care insurance. If you're paying for a family medical policy the amount spent to cover the kids is subtracted from your income before the child support calculation is made.

The amount deducted is determined by dividing the cost of the insurance by the total number of family members it covers. Then multiply that "per person cost" by the number of children subject to child support. For example, assume you pay $3,000 a year to insure yourself and your three kids. The income deduction is found by dividing 4 (you plus 3 kids) into $3,000 and multiply the answer ($750) by 3 (for the 3 kids). In this case, you get to subtract $2,250 ($750 times 3) from your income.

And don't forget the impact of spousal maintenance payments (alimony) on income. The income of the parent paying the alimony is reduced by the amount of the alimony payment. At the same time the one receiving the money has to add it to his or her income both for income tax and child support calculations. So if you receive $1,000 a month in alimony add $12,000 ($1,000 times 12 months) to your annual income. Your former spouse gets to deduct $12,000.

What About Daycare?

Daycare can also have a big impact on the amount of child support paid. However, it must be qualified daycare. That's the kind necessary to allow the custodial parent to work or attend school (for approved work skill training). It's got nothing to do with paying the babysitter for a Friday night out with the boys.

Qualified daycare costs increase the total child support figure (the combined amount paid by the mom and dad) dollar for dollar. For example, take the situation of a stay at home mom with two kids. The guidelines may require a combined total child support payment from both parents of $1,500 a month. However, if the mother (the custodial parent) decides to work and pays $500 a month for daycare the required child support figure goes up to $2,000 ($1,500 plus $500).

But we're not done yet. If the spouse is entitled to a federal daycare tax credit, that credit must be subtracted from the total daycare expense before the daycare expense is used in the child support calculation (this is true even if the spouse doesn't actually take the credit). Only the remaining amount is added to the child support figure.

In the above example, if the mom can get an annual daycare tax credit of $1,200 ($100 a month) the total monthly childcare requirement will only go up to $1,900 ($1,500 plus the $500 daycare expense minus the $100 tax credit).

Doing the Deed

Is anyone out there still following all this? There are lots of other details that can affect the final calculation, but the above are the most important ones. So let's move on to the last step.

At this point it finally gets simple. Taking into consideration all the issues discussed above, the magistrate fills in the guidelines form and determines the total amount of child support required. Then each parent is ordered to pay a share of this child support figure in the same proportion that each parent's income is to the total family income.

Take the case of a husband and wife who have adjusted incomes of $20,000 and $40,000 respectively for a total of

$60,000 a year. Assume the total child support amount figures to be $600 a month. Normally, the husband will be ordered to pay $200 a month, since $200 is one third of $600 ($20,000 is one third of $60,000). The wife then pays the remaining two thirds, which is $400 a month ($40,000 is two thirds of $60,000). That's all there is to it.

Still Room to Maneuver

Well maybe there is a little more to it. Unfortunately, the world is not as uniform as Vermont's Child Support Guidelines. Therefore, magistrates often make adjustments to the child support calculation based on real world circumstances. The good news is that these adjustments may be made up or down depending on the situation. The bad news is that adjustments are becoming the rule rather than the exception.

Let's say the children's standard of living prior to the divorce was above average. The guidelines may not provide enough money to maintain that standard. If the magistrate believes the non-custodial parent can give a higher level of support the court is likely to order payments above the guideline amount. Other above-normal child expenses due to medical or personal needs can also boost the payment.

Of course, if neither parent is capable of funding the prior standard of living then the payments will probably stay within the guidelines. All family members simply have to make a downward lifestyle adjustment. This happens all the time. The court's intention is not to have one spouse enjoying a mansion while the other lives in a camper.

Despite these variations, the guideline formulas provide a pretty good idea of the amount each parent should

expect to pay. They can be obtained from the OCS, the
Family Court or your lawyer.

Where Did All the Money Go?

While the court carefully calculates the child support
amount, no one in Vermont appears very concerned
about how the money is used. The custodial parent can
essentially dispose of it as he or she wishes. There is no
requirement to show that it was spent on the kids.

Also, while the state will aggressively prosecute a non-
custodial parent for failure to pay child support (so-
called deadbeat dads or moms), custodial parents never
have to prove that they made any required payments.
The court simply assumes that they did.

For example, an unemployed mom (the custodial parent) living with her boyfriend was given an imputed
income of $2,000 a month after adjustments (remember
the word "imputed" means that the magistrate is assuming she could earn that income if she was working).
This happens to be 30% of the combined adjusted
incomes of the two parents. Therefore, the magistrate
orders her to pay 30% of the total child support amount
of $1,200 a month. So her monthly payment becomes
$360 (30% of $1,200) and the dad (the non-custodial parent) is ordered to pay the remaining $840 (70%).

But, the mom decides to enjoy her new lover rather than
get a job. Of course it's impossible for her to make the
$360 support payment. Instead, she just learns to get by
on the $840 a month coming in from the non-custodial
parent.   Unless there are clear indications of child
neglect, the court will do nothing to change this situation.

Kindness to a Fault

This book frequently suggests that generosity will be rewarded. That's usually, but not always, the case. If the custodial parent is likely to misuse the child support payments, and/or fail to make a fair contribution, the non-custodial parent may want to keep his or her share of the child support payments as low as possible. This reduces the amount of money the custodial parent is able to misuse.

The non-custodial parent can then make additional payments directly to the children for specific purposes or as a general allowance. This also makes it clear to the children that the non-custodial parent is actually contributing to their well-being, something an irresponsible custodial parent may fail to mention.

The Beatles taught us long ago that "money can't buy me love," but that isn't the intention in this suggestion. It is simply to insure that as much money as possible goes to the right place. If the relationship with the custodial parent is a good one, then none of this maneuvering is necessary.

Also, keeping part of the support payment voluntary rather than agreeing to a payment substantially above the guidelines prevents things from getting out of hand if cash flow problems crop up later on and the payments become more difficult to make.

Adjusting the Child Support Payment After the Divorce Is Final

Unlike other parts of the divorce order, the court is very willing to adjust the child support amount and/or the percentages paid by each parent as time goes by. However, you can't nickel and dime the privilege.

Magistrates are only permitted by law to hear cases where a minimum change of 10 percent (up or down) in the payment amount is alleged to be required.

The passage of time alone can often be the reason to seek an increase. That's because most child support orders don't include a COLA (cost of living adjustment) provision. So if you start off getting $1,000 a month, that's what you'll be getting ten years from now unless you periodically request an increase.

Another time-driven factor is the natural reduction in the number of minor children. Child support payments are not automatically reduced as each kid enters adulthood. Left alone, they will continue at the same rate from the day they are issued until the day the youngest child is no longer entitled to them. That means if you have 17-year-old twins and a third child who is 12 the payments will not go down after the first year when the twins graduate from high school. The non-custodial parent must go to court to seek a reduction because the number of minor children went from three to only one.

While it seems logical that a reduction due to this type of situation will be granted, it's not a sure thing. In cases where the parties have been making the same payments for a long time, other factors like the current salaries of the parents, increases in the cost of living and changes to the Child Support Guidelines may result in a determination that no adjustment should be made even though there are fewer kids.

Other opportunities for seeking adjustments include a child becoming chronically ill or handicapped and in need of long term medical support. The same might be true if a youngster takes on an expensive extracurricular activity like training for the Olympics or membership in a traveling hockey team. A very common situation is one where a parent has moved far away and suddenly the cost of visitation (flying the children from coast to coast) skyrockets.

Changes in income can be a combination of good news and bad news. The good news is you got a big promotion. The bad news is that your former spouse wants an increase in child support. This request is not automatically approved by the court. If, however, support payments were kept low at the time of the divorce because you were having money problems, then the magistrate might rejoice at the opportunity to increase the payments based on your recent good fortune. Rarely is any of this a reason to turn down a promotion.

Also, if your new salary represents a much higher percentage of the combined current incomes of the parties than it did at the time of the divorce, the court may increase what you are paying and decrease what your spouse must pay. So even though the total child support figure doesn't change, someone is paying more and someone is paying less.

On the reverse side, the magistrate is often willing to reduce the amount of child support if one of the parents loses his or her job. The key question will be, was the drop in income involuntary? If it was then relief will usually be granted. Of course it can go up again once the situation improves.

If either of the parents have additional children following the divorce, this added demand on their income is taken into consideration by the court when determining if that parent can afford an increase in child support payments. However, in Vermont, the additional expense of these new children cannot be used as a reason to get existing child support payments reduced.

Finally, until the child support order is modified the non-custodial parent is required to pay the child support as currently specified. There are serious consequences if these payments do not continue. Any changes the court makes are usually retroactive to the date the change was first filed.

When Does It All End?

If you have very young children be prepared for child support payments to continue a long time, but not as long as some other places. In Vermont the kids are entitled to child support until they reach the age of 18 or graduate from high school, whichever comes last. New York, for example, extends these payments if a child goes on to a college or trade school. Not so in the Green Mountain State.

In rare cases, child support can end sooner if a teenager establishes a separate residence away from the custodial parent. However, before you stop making payments be sure the Probate Court issues a specific order stating that the child is "emancipated" (meaning he or she is legally free from parental control). In Vermont the minimum age for emancipation is 16 years old.

This doesn't mean that a youngster living away at boarding school is emancipated. As long as he or she returns on breaks, summer vacations, etc. to the custodial parent's home, the child is considered to be in the physical custody of the custodial parent.

How to Save a Lot of Money

It's pretty clear that child custody is often a long term project. Many changes are going to take place over the years. One solution is to fight every new issue out in court. This becomes a very profitable business for the attorneys. A smarter approach would be to review the situation with your former spouse on a regular basis. When changes are necessary decide on these adjustments out of court.

But remember, any significant alteration agreed to by the parties needs to be submitted to the court. The court will then issue a modification to the child support order. This will allow the court to enforce these changes in the future if necessary.

Let's take a look at a Rawsonville couple to see how this works. The court issued an order for Walter to pay Dorothy, his ex-wife, $900 a month in child support for their son Danny. Shortly after the divorce Walt is laid off and Dorothy verbally agrees to accept a reduced support payment of $500 a month.

Twelve months later Walter is reemployed and back earning his prior salary. He offers to start paying the full $900 again, but Dotty says that's not good enough. She goes to court demanding a year's worth of the shortfall in support payments ($400 a month for 12 months). Since the original support order had never been modified the court will force Walter to make up the difference between what he paid ($500 a month) and what the court order says he should have paid ($900 a month). That's $4,800!

If Walter had gotten the order modified at the time he first became unemployed this problem would have been avoided. When both sides are in agreement, getting the court to issue such a modification is not time-consuming or expensive.

In the end, the money saved on lawyers by a couple working things out between themselves is far better spent on the children. And don't you think the youngsters know that too?

CHAPTER 7

Paternity and the Status of Children

What's This All About?

All children are supposedly created equal, but that's just not true when it comes to a divorce. In the upside down world of "modern lifestyles," it's common for families to contain kids from several different marriages, live together romances, and one night stands. Paternity matters are not only important for divorcing couples, but for ones that have never been married as well.

The status of these youngsters has an impact on two critical issues. The first has to do with parental rights and responsibilities (P R & R) and parent-child contact (P-C C). The second is the amount of child support ordered and who pays it. In a divorce involving children the resolution of P R & R and P-C C is built into the divorce process. However, when the parents are not married a separate paternity action must be filed with the Family Court.

When you think about it for a minute there is some sense to the following argument. If a spouse or unmarried partner is not the legal parent, why should that person have any rights to manage or visit a child (P R & R and P-C C) after the divorce?   And why should that same party be required to support a child that isn't legally his or hers?   Of course, if you think about it a little longer a different conclusion is also possible. More on that later.

Some of this discussion is covered in other parts of the book. However, it's really important and worth visiting again.

Daddy, Daddy, Who's the Daddy?

Everything starts at the beginning. The first step in sorting out the children is determining who are and who are not the parents. This is usually done by having both parties (in either a divorce, live together split up, or one night stand situation) stipulate to the court that they are indeed the parents (natural or adoptive) or legal guardians.

If the divorce involves kids from prior relationships, the stipulation indicates which children are the legal responsibilities of only one of the spouses. But, if paternity is being disputed, then it's time for science to step in and settle the issue.

In the old days a blood test was used to identify the mom and dad. However, that test always left room for doubt. Today, DNA testing is the preferred method. This is the same type of test that proved O. J. Simpson "did it." Oh yeah, that's right, he was innocent.

Anyway, testing DNA samples from both spouses and the children will leave no doubt in a Vermont court as to who are the parents. And you can't refuse to contribute a DNA sample when the judge orders it.

It's Now or Never

This is the time to bring up a sensitive subject. Sometimes a child is born to a married couple and the husband suspects he may not be the biological father. This feeling can exist for years during the marriage without requiring any action. However, a decision point is reached at the time of the divorce. The husband must request a DNA test or he's deemed to be the father.

Once the husband is presumed to be the father there is no going back. If a few months or years later it becomes known that someone else is the father it's too late. The husband will not be released from his child support obligations. So if there are any doubts, the time to express them is during the divorce process.

In some cases the husband has no doubts, but nevertheless down the road finds out he is not the father. Again, it's too late to change things. The same is true for live together and one night stand couples. In all cases, once the parentage order is issued by the judge it cannot be reversed. The court's goal is to create stability and finality in the life of the child.

Our Little Babies

Let's start with the most straightforward situation. Children for whom both the divorcing spouses are the legal parents get all the divorce benefits. In other words, both parents have a chance to get P R & R and P-C C. And they both have an obligation to provide child support based on their ability to pay.

The court will do all it can to insure that these children have a stable home life, maintain a reasonable standard of living and get the benefit of both parents remaining in their lives. Everything discussed under the child custody, visitation and support chapters applies to these youngsters.

The Other Little Ones

Then there are the children parented by only one of the spouses. These one spouse children (stepchildren) might be living full time with the divorcing couple or perhaps only part time (spending the rest of the time with their other parent). The other parent may or may not be providing child support. Perhaps the other parent is dead.

Regardless, the spouse without a legal tie to the children usually has no child support obligation after the divorce. For example, suppose the only children in the family of a divorcing couple were parented by the husband during a former marriage. Following the current divorce his most recent former wife, not legally related to the children, isn't required to pay child support.

Also, she will usually have no custody or visitation rights even if she acted as the primary caregiver (an exception to this is discussed later in this chapter). It goes without saying that the wife's parents who acted like grandparents also get nothing. But grandparents rarely have any rights regardless (see the chapter on grandparental rights).

Finally, if the husband has sole custody of these children (based on the final order of his prior divorce or due to the death of his earlier spouse), then it's likely that he will be awarded the marriage home in the current divorce. After all, he is going to be the primary caregiver in the future regardless of who did that job during the marriage.

The Brady Bunch

Things become more complicated if the divorcing family contains kids from both earlier marriages and the current, soon to be ended, union.

In this case the court focuses first on the children who are the joint product of the divorcing couple. In general, things proceed as if the other kids don't exist. Custody to these jointly produced children normally goes to the parent who was the primary caregiver. All the other P R & R and P-C C issues are settled as described elsewhere in this book.

But there are a few additional twists. When the magistrate looks at each spouse's ability to pay child support, consideration will be given to the fact that one or both parents may have additional children from prior relationships to support as well. The judge applies the same thought process when determining spousal maintenance and property distribution.

For example, a Newport couple had two children from their present marriage (Marty and Buzz) and the wife had two more from a prior marriage (Kathy and Sheri). The magistrate will consider only Marty and Buzz when determining the child support payment. The portion of the total support payment the wife will be asked to pay is reduced because she also has to support Kathy and Sheri.

The income calculation is also affected. The magistrate will reduce the wife's earnings by the amount of child support payments she makes for children from an earlier marriage. On the other hand she may be receiving alimony from a previous husband. If so, that amount gets added to her total income (child support she gets for kids from an earlier marriage is not added to her income). This income figure is an important number when determining the support payments and property distribution.

Children Out of Wedlock

In paternity actions (live together and one night stands) the children are dealt with much the same as in a divorce. However, there are a few differences.

The unmarried mother of a toddler is a bit more likely to be awarded physical custody than would a divorcing woman (in both cases mothers with toddlers are more likely to get custody versus the fathers). But, as the youngsters get older both parents have an equal opportunity to gain custody. As in a divorce, the decision will be based on who has been the primary caregiver, etc. A dad or mom not living at home doesn't stand a chance.

Parent-child contact rights are also similar to those in a divorce. The non-custodial parent is entitled to visitation rights that are in keeping with the best interests of the children. If a parent has been away for a long period of time and suddenly reappears demanding P-C C the court may structure a visitation schedule that gradually increases as the parent-child relationship builds. Grandparents have no more rights in this case than they do during a divorce. They have virtually none.

The child support guidelines for out of wedlock kids are identical to those employed during a divorce. The method for determining how much each parent will pay is also the same.

If the child is a toddler the final order will likely grant the non-custodial parent limited visitation due to the child's young age. Despite the fact that kids eventually grow up, this initial visitation schedule is not automatically subject to simple alteration in the future.

The best way to address this problem is to request that the judge state in the order that visitation must be reviewed at a specific point in the future (when the child is 5 years old, begins school, etc.). If the issue can be resolved in the shorter term the court can be asked to issue an interim order that delays the final order for usually up to six months. This is the type of issue where a lawyer can be very useful.

One last point. Until a decision is made by any court, the mother (unless she objects) is presumed to be the guardian and will have physical custody over all the children.

Enter the New Kids

It's amazing how Vermont's population barely changes while people seem to be having kids left and right. The ink hardly dries on the final divorce order before one or both of the newly freed spouses are out creating another family (in or out of wedlock). Sometimes this happens before the final order!

Don't go to court crying, "Your honor, since the divorce I have remarried and have two new children (referred to as after born children). I can no longer afford to pay as much child support for the kids from my first marriage." You can't use your new kids as reasons to seek a decrease in child support payments.

But, what if the custodial parent takes you to court looking for a child support increase? In this case the new kids count. A magistrate will consider the expense of these after born children when deciding if the non-custodial parent is in a position to pay additional child support. So the new kids will not help reduce a payment, but they can work against having the payments increased.

Vermont Abandons No Child

It may seem like the court is abandoning the children who are not the joint product of the marriage. Nothing could be further from the truth. The judge is simply sorting out responsibilities. Children from an earlier marriage should already be funded under the child support ruling from that earlier divorce.

Only parents or legal guardians can be required to pay child support. If there is no second legal parent (or he or she can't be found) and money is scarce, it becomes an issue for the welfare agencies. They insure that all Vermont children receive the necessary basics.

There Is an Exception to Every Rule

Just when everything is starting to become clear let's throw a wrench into the washing machine. A spouse who isn't the legal parent or guardian of a child may still be entitled to some P-C C rights. That's because the court always puts its concern for the children first.

Imagine a couple in Cambridgeport who have been married for nine years. The husband gained sole custody of a 2-year-old named Barbara following the end of his prior marriage. During his current marriage the wife was Barb's primary caregiver. The little girl, now 11, grew up thinking of this woman as her surrogate mother. In fact, her real mother lives in Arizona and rarely sees Barbara. The divorcing wife desperately wants to continue to have contact with the child.

The court is likely to grant visitation privileges to the wife even though she has no legal responsibility for Barbara. This is not to help the wife, but because it benefits the child. Clearly there is a significant bond between the wife and this girl. However, sole custody would continue to stay with the father. Even though the wife can visit and/or communicate with Barbara after the divorce there is no requirement for her to pay child support.

The reverse can also be true. If the wife was both the parent and the primary caregiver, the other spouse who was not the legal parent is likely to get some visitation rights if he seeks them. Over the nine years of marriage he built up an important relationship with Barbara.

Keep in mind that the visitation rights for these non-parent relationships will normally not be as extensive as they are for the actual parents or legal guardians. It might be as little as the right to send and receive letters or as much as occasional visits to the child's house. After all, the two birth parents are also looking to share time with the youngster.

Nevertheless, on rare occasions stepparents have received more extensive visitation rights. In fact, if neither biological parent is deemed to be fit the judge might award physical and/or legal custody of the child to a stepparent even if he or she has not adopted the child. It's true, the court places the right of such a stepparent to get the kids ahead of the rights of the grandparents.

Children Versus Chevrolets

So far we have been talking about the law. But the statutes cannot cover everything.

A child is not an automobile. There has to be more to the procedure than checking out the registration and moving it from one garage to another. Children enter into their own private contracts with their parents, stepparents and any adult who cares for them. These are not the legal kind of agreements, they are the human kind.

In all aspects of divorce the recommended approach is to settle things between the parties outside the courthouse. But, if you are only going to follow this rule one time, then do it when resolving issues related to the care and support of a child. Whether or not someone is the legal parent doesn't really matter.

No child should have to wake up one day and discover that the person he or she depends on for guidance, nurturing and support is suddenly off limits. Or to learn that this adult could not care less about seeing or supporting him or her ever again. Sometimes the obligations of marriage and divorce extend beyond the law and go directly to the heart.

CHAPTER 8

Grandparental Rights

Banning Grandma and Grandpa

When a divorce is in the works, grandparents often worry about losing contact with their grandchildren. Tensions can mount if the custodial parent is looking to get rid of "those in-laws." Also, custodial and non-custodial parents can sometimes create obstacles for their own parents.

As harsh as it sounds, there may be good reasons to keep the grandparents away. Suppose they are abusive or do drugs or drink too much. Perhaps, they endorse a lifestyle that goes against what the parents are trying to instill in the children. Just because people are older doesn't mean they're automatically wiser. On the other hand, restricting the grandparents could mean that one or both of the parents is simply petty, vengeful, and self-centered.

A Special Note on Marriage and Divorce

The laws covering grandparental rights apply equally during the marriage and the divorce. If married parents want to keep the grandparents away the same rules apply. And the grandparent's legal options are the same as well.

Nevertheless, a pending divorce often brings simmering bad blood to a boil. Issues that were put up with during a marriage to keep peace in the family are no longer tolerated. It doesn't matter who's at fault. The divorcing parents are reorganizing their lives and the grandparents sometimes get caught in the crossfire.

Parents Know Best

The bottom line is that, in Vermont, grandparents have very few rights. Actually, you could say they have none. Yet, it's possible in certain situations for them to get court-ordered visitation. That's because Vermont law revolves around what's best for the kids. So, these children's rights may result in the grandparents gaining some privileges.

Now, all grandparents are immediately going to argue that keeping them off limits is surely not in the best interest of the children. Maybe so, but before a Vermont court will agree there is a major hurdle to overcome.

That big bump in the road is called "parental preference" and it ties right into the court's goal of looking out for the kids. The logic behind parental preference is that parents usually know what's best for their children (at least that's what the court believes). During the marriage both parents have essentially a 50-50 vote on what the grandparents can and cannot do. Obviously, it gets pretty messy if one is against certain grandparents and the other wants them around.

Rights and Permission

After the divorce things change in an important way. The divorce order will specify how and when each parent can be with the children. During his or her specified time a parent has 100% control over whether the grandparents may interact with the kids.

When a parent allows the grandparents to see the children a grandparental right is not being granted. The parent is merely giving them permission to do so. A right is enforceable by the court. Permission is controlled by someone who has a right (normally the custodial and non-custodial parents). It can be here today and gone tomorrow.

The only way for one parent to block the other parent from granting such permission is by showing the court that the grandparents represent a danger to the children. Assuming the grandparents are not Bonnie and Clyde, what exactly are the limits of permission?

The Divine Little Miss "L"

Let's take a look at a precocious nine-year-old named Lisa who lives in Londonderry with Kathryn, her custodial parent. Mark, the non-custodial parent, lives nearby. He has visitation rights totaling two nights a week, plus every other weekend and four weeks during the summer. But Kathy has a "thing" about Mark's parents, Joe and June (J & J), and refuses to allow them to see little Miss "L."

There's a lot Mark might do to help out J & J. To begin with, he can have his parents visit with Lisa at his home during visitation periods. There's also nothing to stop him from bringing Lisa to his parents' house to visit or even to spend the night. And when Mark runs late at work and asks Joe to pick up the little girl at the custodial parent's home for her scheduled overnights can Kathryn stop him? Nope.

In fact, if Mark leaves town for a few weeks he might even ask J & J to fill in for him. They can pick up Lisa at Kathryn's house and take her to their home and return her when the visitation time is over. Mark doesn't have to be around. And, as long as he agrees, J & J can take the little Miss "L" to Disney World during one of the four weeks Mark has her in the summer.

When the Trouble Begins

Okay, so far so good, but what if Mark dies. Joe and June only want to exchange e-mails with Miss "L," but Kathryn forbids it. J & J go to court and the judge accepts Kathy's parental preference. No e-mails, no overnights and definitely no Disney World.

As you can see from this example, the trouble usually begins when the parent who favors the grandparents is no longer in the picture. This can be due not only to death but for several other reasons. Maybe Mark loses his own right to see the youngster (drugs, abuse, etc.), or perhaps he just doesn't care.

If Mark thinks Lisa is an anchor around his neck, he might not seek visitation for himself and couldn't care less whether his parents see the child. One day Mark takes off and fails to leave a forwarding address. J & J could wait a long time before he gets around to giving them permission for anything.

Clearly, there is a big difference between having a right and having permission. If Mark's parents had visitation rights, they wouldn't need anyone's permission to see the child. Still, most grandparents don't have visitation rights and rely on permission. After all, that's how it normally works when couples are married. Parents, in most cases, happily grant this permission, while gaining the assistance and support that grandparents usually provide in great quantity.

Get It in the Court Order

But, if both parents are not completely in agreement with respect to all the grandparents seeing the children an attempt should be made to work things out privately at the time of the divorce. Frequently, more can be gained in this manner than by having the court address the issue.

Make sure that whatever agreement is reached gets included in the divorce order. Putting it in this document transforms the grandparents' permission to see the kids into their right to see them. Later on, these rights can be enforced by the court should it become necessary.

During the negotiation with the parents don't forget to cover the little details. For example, some families have a reunion every few years that the kids need to attend, or the grandparents want the children to be at extended family weddings. They may want to be able to contact the school to find out how the kids are doing and to attend athletic and other events involving the children. Many wish to send Christmas and birthday gifts, exchange letters, e-mails and pictures. And don't forget Disney World.

Would anyone deny such things to the grandparents? The answer is that some parents do for a variety of valid and less than valid reasons!

What Goes Around, Comes Around

It's a particularly difficult situation when both parents refuse to grant permission for grandparental visitation. Still things are not entirely hopeless. Remember the primary rule, "All actions are done which are in the best interest of the children." So for the judge to overrule parental preference and grant a "right" to the grandparents, the grandparents must clearly show that banning them will harm the kids. While this seems pretty straightforward, winning that legal argument isn't easy. Judges are very reluctant to ignore the preference of the parents.

If the grandparents spent little time with their grandchildren during the marriage it's unlikely that the court will consider their plea for visitation rights after the divorce.

On the other hand, children often live with their grandparents for weeks or months while the divorce process is under way. During these periods important stabilizing relationships develop. Similar bonding can occur if the grandparents provided regular daycare support while the parents worked. A judge might be persuaded that it's in the best interest of the children to continue these relationships.

Asking For Guardianship

Sometimes grandparents want the whole enchilada and seek to be appointed as guardians. A guardian has the power to make all legal decisions for the children. This includes deciding where the kids live, where they go to school, etc. You can imagine that such guardianships are granted only under extreme circumstances.

Such a circumstance would be if the custodial parent is, or becomes, unfit to take care of the children (drug addiction, abuse, mentally unstable, depressed, etc.). Another reason is if the custodial parent dies or can no longer perform the functions of parent (severe physical disability, etc.).

In both these situations custody generally goes to the other parent. However, the judge may feel that living with the non-custodial parent is not in the best interest of the children. Maybe the non-custodial parent has the same vices as the custodial parent, or perhaps he or she doesn't want custody.

Guardianship will never be granted simply because the grandparents feel that the parents don't have enough money to adequately provide for the child. Vermont offers a full range of welfare, healthcare, and childcare programs. No judge is going to believe that parents living in Vermont (working or not working) are unable to support their children.

Finally, guardianships represent a temporary status. It can be removed later on if the situation with either or both the parents improves. In rare cases where neither parent wants custody of the children (abandonment) the grandparents can seek to adopt the children. This is done almost always with the consent of the parents. Unlike a guardianship, adoption is permanent.

The Right Time and the Right Court

Grandparental visitation rights are usually not argued during the divorce proceedings, though they can be included in the divorce order if the parents agree. Assuming an agreement with the parents cannot be reached then the grandparents have to go to Family Court on their own once the divorce is finalized. An indication of the limited rights of the grandparents and the general sympathy of the court is that a decision that goes against the grandparents in Family Court cannot be appealed.

Obtaining guardianship of the children is a different process. Guardianship is decided by the Probate Court and never the Family Court. If the grandparents feel the parents are unfit they may seek the support of Vermont's Department of Children and Families (DCF). This state department has the responsibility to protect children who are abused, neglected, etc. Under the DCF's CHINS (Children in Need of Supervision) program a guardianship can be awarded to anyone the court feels is appropriate. Of course this would be done only if both parents were clearly unacceptable. Adoption due to abandonment is also under the jurisdiction of the Probate Court.

Frankly, it's rare for any Vermont court to overrule parental preference regarding a grandparent's visitation rights. It is even less likely (almost never) that grandparents will obtain guardianship of the children. However, if the situation has merit it wouldn't be the first time that the court granted such requests.

The Big Court Speaks Up

It's also rare for the U.S. Supreme Court to become involved in Family Court matters, but it did just that a few years ago. In the majority opinion, Justice O'Connor confirmed the sanctity of the family unit (parents and children) and the court's desire to protect this family unit from the intrusion of the state (all 50 plus the federal government) and the in-laws (grandparents). This underscores the limited rights that grandparents have. It also suggests that any rights granted to them by state legislatures and state courts might not be constitutional.

Everything comes down to the fundamental philosophies of what is best for the children and parental preference. There are exceptions, but they are few and far between. The best solution for grandparents is to be nice to their daughter and son-in-law or son and daughter-in-law before the divorce so they will be welcomed after the divorce.

CHAPTER 9

Spousal Support

The Long and Short of a Marriage

Whether you call it spousal support, maintenance payments or simply alimony there is no doubt that many people have strong opinions on the subject. This controversy reflects the real and imaginary complications that surround the process to determine how much if any support is paid, who will pay and for how long.

First, let's go over how a marriage will be viewed by the court. Basically, it's all about time. There are "short marriages" and "long marriages." The kind you're in has a major influence on the decision making process.

Just how long is long? When does a short marriage become a long one? There's nothing in Vermont law that spells it out. A judge once commented at a hearing that a "long marriage was one of at least 7 years." The lawyer questioned, "Why" and she responded "Well, I was married 7 years and that was way too long!" Actually, if a couple has been married for at least 15 years it's normally treated like a long marriage.

Depending on circumstances, as little as 12 years might qualify.

Which Years to Count

There's no such thing as common law marriage in Vermont. Judges usually start counting the marriage years from the date of the marriage. However, it's not unreasonable for the court to include time spent living together before the marriage when determining its length for purposes of calculating alimony (see the chapter on living together). As usual, it's a matter of the specific details and the specific judge. If a judge wants to count those live together years he or she can and will.

The end of the marriage, when determining whether it's long or short, is the date of the judge's final decision. That might be two years or more after the initial separation or divorce filing. Therefore, it's possible to start the divorce process as a short marriage and by the time alimony is being discussed you are a partner in a long marriage.

So, if you're reading this book to evaluate your options, double-check the date on your wedding band. Sticking it out a few more years could greatly improve your financial return in a divorce settlement or it could do just the opposite if you're the one likely to pay the support.

The Property Distribution Connection

The short versus long marriage issue applies equally to alimony and property distribution. So keep this discussion in mind later on when you're reading the chapter about dividing up the Porsche Boxster, the silver service for 24 and that Mad River canoe.

Price Chopper Joins Hannaford

Think of a marriage as being like two companies that merge. In the beginning things have not really combined and the income generated by each now-merged company is easy to separate. Over time the two organizations start to share offices, manufacture both products in the same factory and utilize a common sales force. It's no longer possible to determine which side is responsible for the success or failure of the merger. A Vermont Family Court judge takes a similar view when deciding on alimony.

For example, imagine that a man comes into a marriage owning a Dairy Queen in Thetford Center. His spouse, who just graduated from high school in White River Junction, shows up with only a rusting 1989 Taurus. If the marriage lasts two years the court is going to look at it pretty much like the early phase of the above described corporate merger. Things are just getting underway and it's still pretty easy to figure out the contributions of each side. Alimony is unlikely to be ordered. An exception might be if one party is disabled, etc.

If the same marriage lasts eight years before breaking up things will be different. It's still a short marriage, but since it has gone beyond five years the court is inclined to provide a transition period for the not so well off spouse. This will cost some money.

Assuming the wife doesn't have independent employment, she now has to find a new place to live and a new job. With few opportunities in Thetford Center, a move to a place like Burlington might be required. Perhaps she needs to attend a training program to develop new job skills. The court will expect the husband to support his spouse during this transition. Usually, these alimony payments last between two to five years.

Things get even more interesting if our Thetford Center couple makes it through 15 joyful years before calling it quits. This is a long marriage and the partners are well merged. By now the Dairy Queen has doubled in size and is going strong. It's usually impossible for the judge to know who has done what over those years to create the current earning stream.

Whether or not the wife actually helped out at the Dairy Queen is unimportant. The same would be true if both spouses were employed at a factory, or if one worked and the other didn't. Couples make choices for many different reasons. "You stay home with the kids, honey, which will allow me to work harder and become the production supervisor. After all, we're in this together."

That kind of decision making goes on every day. In the end, the court assumes that the couple worked as a team to achieve their mutual objectives. Both spouses are considered to have an equal stake in the family income.

Sharing the fruits of all this labor can be achieved through the asset distribution process, but it often involves spousal support as well. This is especially true if one spouse will earn much less than the other in the future. In a long marriage maintenance payments can go on for 20 years or more, perhaps for life.

Keeping Up the Living Standard Following a Long Marriage

One of the objectives of the court in a long marriage is for both parties to maintain their standard of living. So, just what is a "standard of living"? Well, it has to do with the lifestyle the couple enjoyed during the marriage. This includes the kind of house they had, the cars they drove, how often they went out to dinner, the clothes they wore, the kinds of vacations they took, etc.

It's not unusual for the party expecting to receive alimony to believe that because he or she had a home with a view in Charlotte and drove a Volvo turbo wagon that the judge is obligated to insure that such a lifestyle continues. This will only happen if it was a long marriage and there is enough income in the pot to essentially pay for two houses in Charlotte and two turbo Volvos and two of all the rest. The total day-to-day expenses after a divorce may not be double the pre-divorce level, but they will be close enough.

The reality is that after most divorces the standard of living for everyone declines. Five bedroom colonials become three bedroom capes. Three bedroom capes get reduced to two bedroom apartments. The judge will try to spread the pain on a more or less equal basis.

The disappointment definitely increases if the couple was living beyond their means. Now it may be shocking to learn, but there are people who actually spend more than they earn. They live by stacking one credit card on top of the other. While this can apparently go on forever during the marriage, the wheels usually come off the wagon big time when the same trick is attempted following the divorce.

God Bless the Children

If kids are involved the situation changes a little. That's because the court is more concerned with maintaining the children's living standard than it is about keeping an equal standard of living between the two spouses. This is generally true regardless of whether it was a short or long marriage.

Alimony shouldn't be confused with child support. If the court is trying to maintain the children's living standard that money will be awarded through child support. However, judges sometimes unofficially take into account the needs of the children when considering spousal maintenance as well.

This doesn't mean that the kids' living standard won't decline if funds are limited. The court recognizes that in most cases the children will be spending time at the non-custodial parent's home as well. Money has to be available to make this second home at least safe, presentable, and able to accommodate overnights with the kids. Nevertheless, preference will be given to the home where the children are primarily based.

The story gets more complicated if there is shared physical custody or split physical custody. In these cases the court is forced to try to balance the income sharing closer to 50-50, since there are two primary homes.

Divorce has a lot of interconnected moving parts. So, read this chapter along with those on child custody and child support to get the total picture of what to expect. After all, it's a zero sum game. The greater the child support payment, the less money available for alimony, the non-custodial spouse, etc.

Nothing Is as Certain as Change

Vermont generally likes things to be straightforward, so spousal maintenance orders rarely include a cost-of-living adjustment (COLA). However, the order may indicate that periodically (after five years or ten years, etc.) the payment increases or decreases by a specific amount. While being simple is nice, over a period of time it's likely that the payment amount (even if there are stepped increases or decreases) may need to be revised.

Reasons for adjusting the payment up or down include such things as one of the parties getting chronically ill (unable to work and/or has to pay a lot of uninsured medical expenses), or the party receiving the mainte-nance payment has married someone with a substantial salary (remarriage of the receiving party doesn't auto-matically terminate alimony), or either spouse has had a dramatic change in income (big raise or wins the lottery) or substantial inflation.

Keep in mind that the court is only responding to events that have disrupted the balance established by the judge at the time of the divorce. This is not an opportunity to do the divorce settlement over again.

How Long Can This Go On?

One starts out thinking that the marriage will last forev-er, but it turns out that it's the divorce that may never end. There are a few general rules to remember regard-ing alimony. If no maintenance payments are ordered at the time the divorce is final, then they can never be ordered at a later date.

For example, if you and your spouse have great jobs when you get divorced there may be no need for alimo-ny. A few years later you not only lose your job, but also get an injury that prevents you from working ever again (not to mention huge homecare bills that are not covered by insurance). Meanwhile, your former spouse has struck it rich by winning $40 million in the lottery. Even if you had a long marriage, don't expect to go back to court and ask for some kind of delayed maintenance payment. It's too late.

Now here is only a slightly different situation, but with a big change in the result. A divorce order grants you $500 a month in alimony for four years. Three and a half years after the divorce settlement you become permanently disabled and petition the court for a maintenance increase to $5000 a month for as long as you are unable to work (which looks like forever). If your former spouse is capable of paying that amount there is an excellent chance the payments will be increased and extended.

The rule is that while alimony is being paid it can be increased, decreased, terminated or extended indefinitely. However, if maintenance was never part of the final order then it's not possible to ever receive alimony. A strong argument can also be made that if the time period for receiving previously ordered alimony has expired that it cannot be initiated again.

One last thing on payment length. Maintenance payments are not guaranteed under Vermont law. If the party paying the alimony dies the payments automatically end. His or her estate is not required to continue making them. The same is true if the spouse receiving the payments dies. Here, too, the alimony terminates.

However, the IRS is not so understanding. The tax agency requires that the settlement specifically states that the payments end with the death of either party. If not, such payments are likely to be viewed as a property transfer rather than alimony. In that case the paying party will lose the alimony tax deduction.

Income Is a Key Factor

It's easy to see how income makes the wheels go round on any alimony settlement. And keep in mind that the term "income" isn't limited to what gets reported to the IRS. Income may also include imputed earnings for spouses who don't work (the amount he or she could earn if employed) and money received from other sources such as a live-in lover. If a spouse is voluntarily underemployed (a doctor who decides to write poetry instead of practicing medicine) the court may set alimony payments based on what he or she could be earning. Also counted is income received under the table or the equivalent of income in barter situations. (See the chapter on determining income.)

However, as mentioned earlier, when there's not enough income to keep up the living standard then adjustments have to be made. If there really is no money, then there is no alimony.

A Maintenance Strategy: The Story of Jim and Josie

Jim and Josie of Craftsbury were married for 15 years when they got divorced. Jim earns $85,000 a year and Josie, who works part time, earns $15,000. The settlement orders Jim to pay Josie maintenance of $2,500 a month for 10 years. About 5 years into these payments Josie, who now works full time, is earning $65,000. Meanwhile, Jim is in a bicycle accident. He can no longer work and lives off of disability insurance and Social Security.

The court is likely to grant a request by Jim to eliminate his alimony payments to Josie for two reasons. The first is that Jim is now living on a greatly reduced income that has caused his standard of living to decline dramatically. The second is because Josie now earns a substantial income and should be self-sufficient.

Going one step further, is it possible for Jim to ask the court to order Josie to pay him alimony? Remember the statement earlier in this chapter. "If maintenance was never part of the settlement then it's not possible to ever receive alimony." In this case it could be argued that alimony was part of the settlement because Jim was paying it to Josie. How the court will rule on this crafty appeal is highly uncertain.

What should Jim have done to better protect himself? Well, at the time of the divorce along with the monthly $2,500 he had to pay to Josie, Jim could have asked that Josie be ordered to pay him one dollar a year for the same 10 year period. That one dollar annual payment is enough to clearly establish Jim's right to an alimony increase sometime in the future as long as he requests it within the 10 year period specified in the divorce decree. Had he done this, it would be much easier to obtain an increase in both the alimony amount and term following the accident.

While judges will not suggest this one dollar arrangement, they often agree to it, especially in the case of long marriages, if one of the parties makes the request. It's a way of insuring against a dramatic turn of events, just like the one Jim experienced.

Other Factors to Consider

This chapter has stressed the importance of the length of the marriage. However, there are other circumstances that come into play when determining spousal support.

For example, take a 15 year marriage where the parties are in their mid thirties. While this is not a short marriage the parties are young enough to start a new life. This is different than a long marriage divorce with spouses in their sixties. Things for this older couple are pretty much set for the rest of their lives. In the first situation the judge may order maintenance for 10 years, whereas for the other one lifetime support could be required. Even short marriages are not cut and dry. There is a real difference between a two year marriage and a nine year marriage.

What if a spouse is young, but unable to work due to a chronic disease or an injury? Use your imagination. What's the fair thing to do?

Also, while it's usually difficult to know who contributed what to a marriage after 15 or 20 years, once in a while it's quite clear. This doesn't entirely change the outcome, but it can influence it.

Everyone needs to have realistic expectations of what a reasonable judge is likely to provide to each side. Better yet, the parties should work out a deal between themselves and avoid rolling the dice in court.

CHAPTER 10

Property Distribution

California Dreaming

Hollywood movie stars always seem to run up against California's community property law when divorce time rolls around. Blondie Bombshell suddenly marries her chauffeur. Two years later they spilt up and now the former Mr. Bombshell has his own chauffeur and a handsome portion of the Bombshell fortune.

Stories like that make people fearful of community property states. So can you breathe a sigh of relief knowing that Vermont takes a different approach called equitable distribution? Depending on your situation and point of view it's either better or worse in the Green Mountain State. Let's compare the two approaches.

Equitable Distribution
Versus Community Property

The terms "property" and "assets" are used interchangeably in this chapter. Both stand for anything having monetary value. This includes cash, stocks, bonds, real estate, automobiles, homes, furniture, jewelry, cows, horses, pension plans, antiques, etc. Property/assets are different from income. Income is an anticipated future cash flow. Property/assets are what remain of the income received in the past.

Under community property law asset distribution is mostly a mathematical calculation. The first step is to determine what assets were acquired during the marriage regardless in whose names they're registered. This is called marital property. The second is to identify what property belonged to each spouse prior to the marriage and add that to assets each may have individually gained during the marriage such as a valuable gift or inheritance given only to that spouse. This total is called separate property. Separate property doesn't include money that was earned through employment or investments during the marriage by an individual spouse. That is part of the marriage property.

All marital property is divided 50-50 under community property law assuming there is no prenuptial agreement, but each of the parties keep 100% of their separate property. So in the case of the Bombshells, the chauffeur gets half of whatever went into Blondie's bank account from work she performed during their two year marriage (at $20 million a picture that was a lot). He also receives half of everything that was purchased with those earnings. However, the chauffeur doesn't get half of her house or jet because Blondie had bought them before the marriage.

Vermont's equitable distribution law requires that the judge look beyond the straightforward calculation of a community property settlement and into what is really fair and just. Fair and just may still mean dividing everything 50-50, but not always. If one side has greater needs than the other, the needy party might get more of the assets. However, neither spouse is automatically entitled to anything. It depends on the situation.

This is the big difference compared to a community property ruling that doesn't consider the other aspects of the divorce when dividing the assets. Under community property law the judge can't modify the asset split. It is virtually always 50-50 for the marriage property and 100% to whomever has rights to the separate property.

Had Blondie and her chauffeur-husband lived in Vermont he might not get millions of dollars for such a short marriage. He did nothing to earn it and doesn't need it to survive. If it was a long marriage it could be a different story. This "judgment call" aspect of an equitable distribution ruling makes it more difficult to predict how the court will divide the assets compared to a community property state.

Vermont, One of the Most "Flexible" States

Actually, there are only eight community property states in the U.S. The others, like Vermont, use some variation of equitable distribution. Is anyone surprised to learn that Vermont takes the broadest and most flexible approach in this regard?

Many equitable distribution states separate assets into marital property (everything acquired during the marriage with a few exceptions) and separate property (everything acquired prior to the marriage with a few additions). However, states vary on how they deal with these two categories.

Vermont doesn't separate assets into the marital and separate classifications. Sure, if it's a short marriage much more consideration will be given to the original source of each asset. However, the rules allow any asset to be given to any party if the judge believes it's the fair and just thing to do.

While it may be comforting to learn that the goal in Vermont is to be fair and just, that isn't everyone's personal objective. If you are the less needy spouse it's possible that you will get less than half the assets. Clearly you should have been living in California.

12 Famous First Questions

Ask any good Vermont divorce attorney the basis for an equitable distribution property settlement and instantly he or she will rattle off the following twelve key questions that all judges must factor into their final decision.

1. The length of the marriage

Was it a short marriage where the efforts and assets of the two parties are easy to separate? In a long marriage it becomes harder to know the value of each party's contribution. The longer the marriage the more likely the court will assume that both parties contributed equally to the assets of the partnership. (See the discussion on long and short marriages in the spousal support chapter.)

2. The age and health of the parties

Is each spouse young enough and healthy enough to go out and rebuild an asset base? What if one is old, disabled and/or chronically ill? That makes a big difference in what the court decides.

3. *The occupation, source and amount of income of each of the parties*

The more lucrative and in demand the occupation, the easier it is for the party to re-establish important assets. However, a spouse's income doesn't have to come from a job. It might come from things like trust funds and investments.

4. *Vocational skills and employability*

How easily could a party who is not currently employed return to the workforce? Also, based on skills and experience, how much is he or she likely to earn?

5. *The contribution by one spouse to the education, training, or increased earning power of the other*

There's no free lunch. All those days one spouse was going to law school while the other worked to support the family is important to the court. The same goes for the time one spouse put his or her career on hold so the other could take a four year assignment in Singapore and get that big promotion. The supporting spouse helped create that hefty income stream even if the other spouse is earning the money. One way to reward the helpful spouse is with a generous share of the assets or with spousal support payments or a combination of both.

6. *The value of all property interests, liabilities, and needs of each party*

This largely refers to an inventory of what is owned, as well as what is owed. What special needs dictate who gets what? The person whose name is actually on the deed, title, etc. makes little difference. In the eyes of the court it's all available for distribution to either party.

7. Whether the property settlement is in lieu of or in addition to maintenance (alimony)

Often there is not enough income to provide a fair amount of alimony. One way of making up for this shortage is to give the under-supported spouse a larger portion of the property. The judge may decide to award more assets, but reduce or deny alimony.

8. The opportunity of each spouse for future acquisition of capital assets and income

This is another way of looking at what some of the other questions touch on. What chance does either spouse have to move up the corporate ladder? Some might never even find the ladder. The judge will also be thinking about the assets necessary for retirement.

9. The desirability of awarding the family home, or the right to live there, for reasonable periods to the spouse having custody of the children

This specifically deals with who gets the family home. It doesn't necessarily separate the family home from the rest of the assets when considering what is a fair division. If the custodial parent gets the house its value is factored into the judge's decision regarding how the remaining property is divided. Also, just because a spouse gets the family home doesn't mean that all the equity (home value less the mortgage) goes to that spouse. The equity is often split between the parties.

10. The party through whom the property was acquired

Who brought what into the marriage? The court considers what each party owned before they married. It also looks at things like an inheritance or a valuable gift that was received by one of the parties during the marriage. In short marriages this is very important. In long marriages the judge usually looks at everything as being equally owned. However, an inheritance, gift, or the like received by only one of the parties near the time of the divorce is less likely to be divided.

11. The contribution of each spouse in the acquisition, preservation, and depreciation or appreciation in value of the respective estates, including the non-monetary contribution of a spouse as a homemaker

Did both sides contribute equally to create the marriage property? "Equally" doesn't only refer to an equal contribution of income. It specifically points out that the efforts of a homemaker with no income must be considered. On the other hand, a spouse who ran out five years ago, leaving the other spouse to pay for everything, may be out of luck.

12. The respective merits of the parties

What was the conduct of each party during the marriage? Did one party commit adultery or abuse the other? Was either spouse drunk all the time and/or fail to work steadily inside or outside of the home due to a lack of effort? Is it payback time? Maybe, but probably not.

So What's It All Mean?
Anyone reading the above 12 questions jumps on the ones that are in their favor. "I did all the work. If it wasn't for me there would be nothing to split up." "That bum has been cheating on me since the honeymoon." "I stayed at home raising the kids, how can I start earning a living at my age?" And so on and so on.

The first thing to realize is that not all the questions have the same importance. Spouses who put up with lying, cheating and drunkenness for 20 years are surprised to find that personal behavior (question 12, "merits of the parties") is at the bottom of the totem pole in Vermont. Remember, punishing a spouse isn't the judge's main objective. Your wishes may differ from the court's on this point.

If there is not enough income to support the costs related to child support and alimony, then the judge will look to use the property to cover that shortfall. Despite the term equitable distribution, the prime objective is not to insure that the assets are equally split.

Whether it's a fine antique silver service or "the best damn fishing camp this side of Lake Champlain," the court views assets simply as a source of money (when sold) to meet the financial demands of the divorce. Often there is little left after that.

Now, the court usually doesn't micromanage the settlement. It normally allows each party to figure out how the financial obligations caused by the divorce decree will be met. However, when the final order states that the non-custodial parent must give the custodial parent a certain amount of cash, or monthly alimony, the judge knows that the only way this can be done is for the non-custodial parent to sell some property.

The same is true if extra assets are awarded directly to the custodial spouse and/or a spouse receiving less than the usual amount of alimony for a certain situation. The judge assumes that the property will be sold to generate more income. There is something just so "Vermont" about this process!

Regardless of how rich or poor the parties are the court will have the same priorities. Children come first, spousal support payments, if required, are second and everything else is third. However, there still needs to be a balance in the final order. A judge is not going to give everything to the kids and a needy spouse so they can maintain a high living standard, while the other spouse is left to starve.

When money is tight everyone is expected to sacrifice, and this is very often the case. Few people gain financially through divorce. Frequently, both sides lose a lot of ground as they discover it was much cheaper living together.

The Long and Short of It

If there are still some assets remaining after taking care of the kids and alimony, then whether the marriage was long or short becomes really important. This issue is discussed in the chapter on spousal support and also the one on living together. Here's a brief summary.

A long marriage is one that lasts 15 years or more, but sometimes as little as 12 years. If a couple lived together for a period of time and then got married and after a few more years are now getting divorced the issue is more complicated. The court can include the live together period when determining if it was a short or long marriage. It's up to the judge and the situation, so don't count on it.

How Things Get Split Up

In a short marriage it's more likely that the assets will be split in a manner similar to the community property rules with marriage property shared 50-50 and separate property going to the relevant spouse (take a look at the start of this chapter for clarification of these terms). The shorter the marriage the more this is the case.

With long marriages it's assumed that all the assets are jointly owned regardless of whose name they are owned under or who brought what into the marriage. There is also the understanding that each spouse has an obligation for the long term welfare of the other.

The judge evaluates each party's job skills, work history, and earning capability. More property may go to the spouse that is likely to have trouble building up an asset base in the future. To understand this logic consider the following situation.

An Essex Junction couple in their mid-fifties is getting divorced. The wife has never been employed while the husband is earning a good income at IBM. Even if the unemployed spouse gets a job the judge may feel that given her age and limited skills the accumulation of significant assets by retirement time is unlikely. Meanwhile, the IBM employee is in a much better position to replace the property he loses due to the divorce. Guess who's going to get more of the assets?

Age has a lot to do with this decision. If the non-working spouse is 35 instead of 55, the outcome might be different. In this case, there's plenty of time for the unemployed spouse to upgrade job skills and develop a career. Of course, if there are five small youngsters at home or the party is in ill health that's less likely to happen. Those factors also affect the final asset distribution.

Bad, Bad Leroy Brown

Have you noticed that question 12, the "respective merits of the parties," hasn't been a factor yet? If it's ever going to be an issue, the behavior must have been physical abuse or created such incredible stress that professional care was required.

Many people believe that adultery has a big influence on the judge's decision, but it rarely does. The moral character of the partners is usually not much of an issue in the final settlement. This is especially true if it occurs after the separation. Many other considerations are more important.

That's not to say a spouse's lack of merit is always ignored. Bad behavior can make the judge feel that the person is not trustworthy, resulting in the final order requiring him or her to pay more things immediately and to have less control over future issues. And if these misdeeds brought about significant suffering the court may indeed award more assets to the injured spouse as compensation.

One little point on adultery. Often, though not always, the adulterous spouse experiences a lot of guilt when first discovered. In this vulnerable state he or she is willing to be very generous in terms of a divorce settlement. This is the time for the other spouse to strike quickly (assuming forgiveness is not an option) and move the divorce through the system as rapidly as possible. Guilt has a way of fading fast.

Taking a Sentimental Journey

Articles that have both monetary and sentimental value (like Grandma's china set) are always part of the total property/asset inventory. However, the judge will usually award such items to the spouse for which it has the greatest sentimental meaning. Such an award is not held separately from the overall division of property. So, if you get the antique hooked carpet you will probably get less of something else.

Items that only have sentimental value are given to the spouse that is most attached to them. But in this case, getting to keep the family cat or selected photos of the kids will have no impact on how the valuables are split up. Unfortunately, if a judge is required to decide who gets to keep things having little economic value it's going to be a long divorce. Everyone really has to try harder!

Speaking of sentimental items, don't forget the engagment ring. It's part of the jointly owned assets even though the ring was a gift from one spouse to the other.

Enter the Tax Man

Spousal support and property are taxed differently. Alimony is taxed as ordinary income for the one receiving it. It's a tax deduction for the one who pays. If the receiving party is in a low income bracket and the paying spouse is in a high one it may make sense to pay more alimony and give fewer assets.

But a receiving spouse in a high income bracket may prefer to get less alimony and more assets.   This is because property is not taxed when it is received. Later on if it's sold the tax is often at the much lower capital gains rate.

Of course this kind of tax planning is not available to couples that leave it up to the court to decide who gets what. Don't expect that kind of detailed thinking from the judge. If taxes are important, then the parties should work out an agreement before going to court.

CHAPTER 11

Property Issues and Considerations

Matters of Life and Debt

Banks, credit card companies and automobile manufacturers own a good portion of what people call their property. We are reminded of this each month as the payments come due. So it's important to consider this debt when valuing assets.

Obviously, a $400,000 farm with a $350,000 mortgage has a value of $50,000 for the divorcing couple. Less obvious is the fact that having debt on an asset automatically reduces its value beyond the money that is owed.

Consider the situation of a couple in Bartonsville getting divorced. The combined value of their assets is $250,000. However, they also have debts totaling $100,000. So, their property represents only $150,000 in equity ($250,000 less $100,000).

The divorce settlement grants each side half of the equity ($75,000 each). However, one party receives assets worth $75,000 having no debt while the other gets property valued at $175,000, but having $100,000 of debt. Which one is better off?

Most people would rather have the assets with no debt attached. Forget, for the moment, the sentimental or practical value certain assets have even if there is debt on them. After the divorce, monthly payments that used to be hard to make may become impossible to make.

Normally a Vermont judge will try to spread the debt between the parties. However, this may not be done equally. As with everything else, the court will consider each side's ability to take on the debt burden.

In the end, it's often necessary to sell the debt-ridden property and pay off the loan. In the case of real estate the selling costs can be substantial. If your hunting camp is worth $45,000 and the debt on it is $15,000, its value in a divorce is $30,000. However, if you have to sell it after the divorce in order to make the alimony payments it will cost you about $1,800 in fees for the broker. The court almost never takes this $1,800 cost into account when doing the split.

Credit Card Mania

As best it can, the court will match up the credit card debt with the items purchased. If a refrigerator was bought using a credit card then whoever gets the refrigerator in the asset split gets that portion of the debt as well. The judge will also look at what expenditures were made after the separation and give that debt to the party who generated it.

The name on the credit card is not as important as who received the benefit from using the card. Anyway, regardless of which spouse signed up for the card, the other spouse is often appointed as an authorized user. In that case the card is legally in both their names.

It's Hard to Escape Debt

If the two parties were legally responsible for a debt before the divorce then both remain legally responsible for it after the marriage from the point of view of the lender. While the court can designate who must pay the debt, there is no way it can remove a spouse's name from a loan obligation. If the spouse assigned the debt by the court fails to make the payments, the lender can legally go after the other party.

Sure, the innocent party may sue the designated spouse for failure to pay. But this takes time and money. And what if the designated party is broke or dies and the estate has no funds to pay off the debt? The innocent party will probably have to make good on all remaining payments.

For example, suppose both spouses sign a loan to buy a used Volvo 240 wagon (that is one great car!). In the divorce settlement the husband gets the Volvo and responsibility for the debt. Unfortunately, the payments stop six months later when he is killed while totaling the car.

If the car was uninsured (another payment he forgot to make), the auto loan company will go after both the former husband's estate and the other spouse to collect the debt. The same would be true if the husband defaults on the loan because he loses his job. It's not the loan company's fault the couple got divorced.

Big money gets involved when the debt in question is a $100,000 mortgage signed by both spouses on the marriage home. The judge will usually try to reduce this risk by ordering the party getting the house to make a good faith effort to refinance it under his or her name only. Proof of this effort may have to be provided every six months until it's successful.

It's smart to request the court to order all debt refinanced under the name of the person responsible for the payments. Unfortunately, just as in the case of the marriage home, banks are often unwilling to write a new loan based on the income of just one spouse.

Admit the Ship Is Sinking

Sometimes you simply can't get from here to there. The cost of child support, spousal maintenance, and paying for two households with an income that barely supported one before the divorce can be overwhelming. Parents need to provide a proper housing and living standard for their kids. Even without children the debt payments can be too much. The only choice may be bankruptcy.

Under bankruptcy law (with some limitations) the parties can keep the homes in which they live, along with their cars, furniture, clothes and a small amount of money. While their other assets will be lost, they would have lost them anyway since there was no way to keep up the payments.

Taxing Questions

Taxes need to be considered when property is being split up. Consider the story of three different assets. The first is a house that was purchased 10 years ago for $75,000 and is now appraised at $125,000. The second is a seasonal camp also purchased 10 years ago for $75,000 and now worth $125,000. The third asset is a portfolio of stocks and bonds that were inherited less than a year ago. At the time of the inheritance they were worth $25,000, but by some miracle they are now valued at $75,000. Now assume that just after the divorce all three were sold.

The $50,000 long term capital gain on the house ($125,000 less $75,000) is not taxed by either the federal or Vermont governments since it was within the capital gains limit and the home was a primary residence for the last two years. (New laws are making it even easier to avoid this tax for divorcing couples.) Meanwhile, the $50,000 long term capital gain on the camp ($125,000 less $75,000) is taxable because the camp was not a primary residence (the federal tax alone could be as high as 15% or $7,500). The $50,000 profit on the stocks and bonds ($75,000 less $25,000) is considered a short term capital gain and will be taxed at the ordinary income tax rate. Adding this short term capital gain to the rest of your regular income could result in a substantial federal tax rate. At 25% (it could be higher or lower) you would be paying $12,500 in taxes. Don't forget that the camp and the stocks and bonds are also subject to Vermont's taxes.

Those are shockingly important differences. Shocking to you perhaps, but not to the Vermont court that often ignores them. So, if the property split is left up to the judge don't expect these tax issues to affect the distribution. One party can get something with tax free equity while another receives something with an equity that is subject to a heavy tax at some point in the future. The judge may call it a 50-50 split, but after taxes are paid it's hardly that.

Lawyers who point this disparity out to the court are often unsuccessful. So, if you're working out a deal directly with your spouse keep the tax impact in mind.

This is another good reason to avoid going to court. It's also a reason to seek professional tax help.

A Special Note About Home Equity

When the judge looks over the property list, often the first item to get split 50-50 is the equity in the marriage home (the difference between what the house is worth today and the mortgage). Even if there are other significant assets the judge may still want the marriage home equity to be shared.

While the court likes to have this equity split take place as soon as the divorce is final, it's not always possible. In this case the judge will allow it to be delayed until the paying spouse is in a stronger financial position. When that time comes the payment will include an interest charge to compensate for the delay.

Various events can trigger this future equity payment including when the "spouse with the house" remarries, has a live-in lover or has a tenant, all of which are assumed to increase available income. It can also be when the house is sold, refinanced or the occupying spouse gets a significant salary increase. The payment is usually never postponed past the day the children are no longer entitled to support.

Traditional Pension Plans

It's understandable that many people don't think the right to a traditional pension, the kind that pays a fixed amount each month after retiring, is property like a home or a bank account. Perhaps, this pension right was initiated prior to the marriage and its value will continue to build well after the divorce. No one knows what it will be worth when it's actually collected. If a person quits or is let go before retirement age the pension value is greatly diminished. Maybe the pension will never be paid since vesting can take several years.

All that is quite true. However, a pension is an asset and it will definitely be on the table when the property settlement is being hammered out. Next to the equity in the marriage home, a pension may be the only other item having any value. How does the court deal with it? Here are a few simple facts.

The first is that a pension is treated by the court just like any other property. Neither side has any special rights to it. Because of its importance with respect to retirement, the judge is likely to split the pension 50-50 rather than give it all to one party.

The second fact is that pension rights are earned over a long period of time, but it's only the specific span of time that the spouse was both married and earning credit towards a pension that counts in determining the distribution. For example, if someone retired from a company after 20 years, but was only married for five years during that time, then his or her spouse would be entitled to share in no more than 25% of the pension (5 years is 25% of 20 years).

A third fact is that while a pension is a promise to pay an uncertain amount of money in the future, there are ways to estimate its current value. To do this an actuary or economist (experts in estimating such values) must be hired to testify in court. Based on this testimony, it's possible that a judge will award up to 100% of this estimated value to one spouse (adjusted to cover only the married years as discussed above). And it would be paid at the time of the divorce, possibly well before the pension actually started paying benefits.

It may seem amazing that the court can order a spouse to pay in advance a portion of a pension that might never be collected. While it certainly does happen, it's not the most common result. One reason for this is the uncertain nature of the estimate. A second reason is that many parties can't afford to hire a highly paid pension expert. In the end, after spending all that money a judge may fail to agree with the expert's proposal. Finally, the spouse with the pension often doesn't have the money to pay the pension's value at the time of the divorce.

Almost always, the judge will order the pension to be shared on a monthly basis at the time it's actually collected. To understand how this would work let's continue with the above example where the marriage represents 25% of the total pension earning period. Assume the working spouse retires and receives a pension amount of $ 1,000 a month and the sharing spouse is awarded half the pension value, a 50-50 split. This works out to the sharing spouse receiving $125 a month ($125 is half of $250 which is 25% of the $1,000).

It's critical for the pension sharing spouse, following the divorce, to immediately notify the company or the agent who manages the other spouse's pension fund of the court order to split the pension. If the spouse earning the pension drops dead before this notification, the pension sharing spouse gets nothing.

The same is true if the spouse who is earning the pension fails to list the other spouse as a beneficiary of the pension should the pension earning spouse die before retiring. So make sure you ask for survivor benefits.

Notification is made using a form called a Qualified Domestic Relationship Order (QDRO). Usually, the party getting the pension share (not the party earning the pension) files this directly with the company or agent. The court is not responsible for doing this.

The QDRO informs the company of the sharing spouse's legal right to a portion of the pension. When the pension earning spouse retires the company will send the appropriate amounts directly to each party every month.

Sometimes the sharing spouse dies before the spouse with the pension retires. In this case, if the QDRO has a reverter clause, the spouse earning the pension can notify the court and it will rescind the QDRO. So make sure a reverter clause is included in the QDRO.

The spouse who earned the pension will now get 100% of the total pension when he or she retires (actually it works out to about 90-95% since the pension is subject to a fee due to the reverter). The estate of the dead sharing spouse has no rights to the pension.

Taking a Look at 401(k)'s and IRA's

The above discussion dealt with a traditional pension plan. It's often called a defined benefit plan because for a given age, salary and years of employment there is an exact amount of money that will be paid out. Plans like this use to be the norm, but not any more.

Today, companies are more likely to offer an alternative retirement plan called a 401(k) which has a defined contribution rather than a defined benefit. Every month the employee and the employer contribute specific amounts into this retirement account. Like the defined benefit plan it's difficult to predict the future value of a 401(k) account since it depends on interest rates, the stock market, the amount contributed, etc.

However, it's easy to know the current value of a 401(k) account and to divide up this amount. So, unlike the situation with a defined benefit plan, the receiving spouse usually doesn't have to wait to get a portion of his or her spouse's 401(k) savings. IRA's and similar kinds of defined contribution plans are dealt with much the same as 401(k) accounts.

When the divorce is absolute, funds can be rolled over into the other spouse's 401(k) account (he or she may need to start one) without paying any penalties or taxes. Of course, if the receiving spouse spends the money rather than rolling it over the normal penalties and taxes will apply.

What About Social Security?

If both spouses have been working it's possible they have similar individual benefits. In this case, the judge ignores the social security issue. However, if one spouse has been a stay-at-home and did not develop separate social security benefits the benefits of the other spouse will likely be considered when the judge is determining the needs of the non-working party.

The Date of Plan Valuation

A final note on valuing pensions. All property, except pensions, is valued as of the date of the final divorce hearing. Pensions are valued as of the date of the separation. That means the date the couple stopped living together.

The reason for this is to encourage the spouse earning the pension to continue to contribute to it. If the pension was valued at the date of the final hearing a spouse might see no incentive in keeping up the contributions when the other spouse was going to end up with a good portion of the money. This is particularly meaningful with respect to 401(k) type plans where the employee contribution represents a large portion of its value.

Dotting the I's and Crossing the T's

While the final order lays out the division of assets, afterwards there is often more work to be done. If lawyers are representing the spouses they will take care of these details. However, when attorneys aren't used things can slip through a crack or two.

The most common issue relates to the marital home. Often the court will award the home to one spouse with the requirement that a specific amount of the equity value is to be paid to the other spouse.

In order to implement this directive the spouse keeping the home must receive from the other spouse a "quit claim deed." In this document the now homeless spouse gives up all rights to the marital home and in return receives from the spouse keeping the house a "mortgage deed" saying the spouse with the house owes him or her the amount specified in the final order. It will also say how that money will be paid (also specified in the final order).

Failure to get such documents executed right away can create lots of problems later on. Yes, most can be resolved, but usually that involves both added expenses and delays. So before running off into the sunset make sure any necessary follow-up documents are signed, sealed and delivered.

CHAPTER 12

Dissolving a Civil Union

Big Dog in a Little Dog's Body

There is nothing small about Vermont's view of its role in the world. The Green Mountain State wants to lead despite a limited geography and tiny population. So it was hardly surprising when civil union legislation went from start to finish in a single year.

Not surprising, but still remarkable. After all, it can take two years or more just to get a building permit. And you may never get it! Indeed, our legislature enjoys making social action history.

Let's Start at the Beginning

There's very little difference between getting married and entering a civil union. In both cases the couple goes to the town clerk's office, fills out a form, pays a small fee and off they go. The ceremony is performed by anyone authorized to join two in marriage.

No residency requirements, no blood test, nothing else. Arrive from out of state on Tuesday morning and leave

Burlington International Airport that evening as blissful civil union partners.

But keep in mind that 50% of all marriages end in divorce. Civil unions haven't been around long enough to have good statistics, but what's your guess on the failure rate? That's right!

Applying the Law

One reason Vermont's notoriously slow legislature was able to create civil unions so quickly was that they piggybacked it onto existing laws and processes. All the rules for obtaining a divorce in Vermont apply to civil unions, including using the Family Court. Not much effort on the part of our state leaders in doing that.

So virtually everything in this book applies to civil unions. That sounds pretty simple. But for non-residents it can create a few curveballs.

Do You Own Snowshoes?

There is no residency requirement for getting married or civil unioned in Vermont, but there sure is one for ending either.

The law requires that at least one civil union partner be a Vermont resident for at least six months before filing for dissolution. That party must continue to live here until the legal split is made final. The catch is that the court won't finalize things unless he or she has spent a minimum of the previous 12 months dwelling in the Green Mountain State.

Remember, the same laws apply to both civil unions and divorce. This includes the possibility of having to resolve all the children issues (no longer unusual in same sex relationships), as well as alimony, and property distribution. The chance for a lengthy disagreement looms large. A final resolution could easily take 12 to 24 months to accomplish. During that entire time one of the partners has to reside in Vermont.

And just how does one demonstrate residency? By getting a driver's license, or registering to vote, or actually living and working in the state. Just having a Vermont postal address is not enough.

Out of state residents shouldn't count on terminating a civil union in their home state. So far only a few other states are willing to recognize and terminate a Vermont civil union.

Has anyone missed the point? Unless you live in the handful of pro civil union states don't expect to end a civil union without someone residing in Vermont for quite a while. Since well over 80% of civil union partners live somewhere else that's important to know.

Test Pilots, Start Your Engines

Very little legal history exists about defunct civil unions. Some believe that there is little risk if the joining fails. As civil unions are not recognized in most states one can just walk away from the deal with no damage done.

Maybe so, but maybe not. Think about two guys from Kansas. David is a successful businessman who has a steady six-figure income, a big house and substantial savings. Robert, his companion, is of far less substantial means. He has nothing.

Skiing in Vermont one winter they decide to get unionized at the local town hall followed by a fast flight back to the Midwest. Several years later the relationship is dead. Robert gets kicked out of the house and heads for Vermont (no same sex marriage or civil unions in

Kansas). Six months go by and then a complaint is delivered to David's door. It seems that Robert is looking to "legalize" the split. He also wants a substantial part of David's savings.

David ignores the notice, assuming that because Kansas doesn't recognize civil unions a Vermont court order isn't enforceable. David doesn't defend himself and Robert gets a pretty good deal in the final order. Soon he's back to Kansas and racing to the courthouse.

Will the Kansas court force David to pay? Is Robert about to jump onto the gravy train? Was David right in thinking that Robert has only a worthless piece of paper? No one can be sure. The law is still developing and in this case David is the test pilot.

Same Tune but Different Lyrics

Let's alter the above situation with Dave and Bobby. They are still ready to split up, but this time Dave is worried about the financial possibilities. Bob definitely is the type to go after as much of Dave's fortune as he can. If things drag on much longer the relationship could be viewed as a long term one. Dave wants to end things now, but that means giving up his job and moving to Vermont or one of the few other states willing to dissolve civil unions .

So he rents an apartment in Burlington, which was harder to find and more expensive than he had imagined, and commutes to work in Kansas. This goes on for two years before getting a final order that tends to favor Robert anyway. Along the way, Dave discovers that Vermont's state income tax is roughly 25% of an individual's federal income tax assessment!

Your Money and Your Life

It's easy to see the difficulty caused by other states failing to recognize civil unions. Less obvious is the danger
if a state unexpectedly recognizes them. That's because
entering a civil union is serious business. It isn't something to do just for fun or simply to make a social statement.

A well publicized case involved a Connecticut resident who desperately tried to end his civil union. It
seems he was close to death and feared his unionized
partner might inherit a portion of this dying man's
estate that he wanted to go to his kids from an earlier
marriage.

The Connecticut court (the surviving partner must seek
the inheritance in the state where the dying man
resided) had not yet made a judgment regarding
Vermont civil unions. One way to force the issue was for
the dying partner to sue for "divorce" in Connecticut. If
the court recognized the civil union he would terminate
it and avoid the inheritance question entirely. Should
the state fail to recognize the union then the other party
would have no legal basis for latching onto part of the
estate.

In this case the Connecticut court didn't recognize civil
unions. But what about other states or even Connecticut
at a later date? In fact, today Connecticut recognizes
civil unions along with some other states that didn't do
that only a few years ago.

Walking around with an uncanceled civil union after the
spark is gone from the relationship is like floating a boat
in a sea full of explosive mines. It looks like the test
pilots will have plenty of missions.

Bye Bye Baby, Baby Goodbye

But it's not only about money. Nontraditional families are looking more like "Leave It to Beaver" all the time and children are a big part of this new lifestyle. Whether through a previous relationship, adoption or the miracle of science these kids arrive on the scene much as they do in a mom and pop marriage.

Of course there is one exception. Obviously, both civil union partners cannot be the biological parents. Maybe one, but not two. So at least one party has to go the adoption route in order to have legal rights to the child in question.

Anyone lacking legal responsibility for a youngster during the civil union will have a hard time claiming visitation rights and no chance at getting custody after it is dissolved. That also means there will be no obligation to pay child support. None of this is much different than in a divorce situation (see the chapter on paternity and the status of children). Just something to keep in mind.

A Sticky Tax Question

You will recall that in long term marriages (usually 15 years or more) alimony is quite possible. Also, remember that judges sometimes combine living together time with the time spent married or in a civil union. Therefore, some long term civil unions might already exist. Regardless, even in short term relationships, alimony is often used for transitioning to the singles life.

Under federal and state laws alimony is a tax deduction for the person paying it and taxable to the receiving party. However, it's less clear how alimony paid as part of a civil union breakup would be treated.

Only Vermont and a few other states have civil union or same sex marriage laws.   Civil union alimony may be viewed by the IRS and your state government as a gift. That means it may not be deductible from the giver's income. At the same time, it may be taxable income to the receiving party to the extent it exceeds the annual gift tax exclusion. Where are those test pilots when you need them?

By the way, child support, regardless of whether it stems from a divorce or a dissolved civil union, is not taxable to the custodial parent.

A Civil Union Prenuptial

One way to reduce the settlement problem is to have a prenuptial agreement just like in a marriage. Such a document outlines what each side's obligation will be to the other in case of a split. When properly done they are easily enforceable by the court. Most states (including those without civil unions) would recognize such a contract as being similar to a partnership agreement.

However, having a prenuptial does nothing to legally dissolve the civil union. In fact, normally these agreements are triggered by getting divorced or, in this case, deunionized, but other triggers could be included. It is possible to implement a prenuptial type agreement without legally dissolving the civil union.

The issue of how to close down a civil union without one side residing in either Vermont or one of the few recognizing states remains. A prenuptial agreement simply reduces the suspense regarding what the final decree is going to be. More work for the test pilots.

Yellow Bird Sits in Banana Tree

Necessity is the mother of invention.

Years ago many people went for quickie divorces to the Caribbean or Mexico. This avoided having to prove adultery or some other behavioral problem as required by many states. It also got around state residency issues like the ones faced by out of state civil unioners. In these tropical jurisdictions things got done in a couple of days.

However, when no fault divorce laws came along the need to leave the country for an easy divorce disappeared. Sadly, this change took a big bite out of the income pie for quite a few beachfront lawyers, palm tree court systems, hotels and airlines.

Could we be looking at a rebirth of this offshore industry in the name of civil unions? It might be fun to jet down to Belize or a similar location for a few days and dump your partner while working on a suntan? Sounds better than one or two years battling snowdrifts and cluster flies in Vermont. No one is saying anything yet, but keep your snorkel handy. Happy hour could be starting up just beyond the beach cabana. Who knows?

The Future of Civil Unions

By now you realize there's a lot more unknown than known about civil unions. Nevertheless, as other states (such as California) develop similar laws they will likely recognize Vermont civil unions just as they recognize Vermont marriages today. This makes the future full of possibilities.

For example, Liliana and Juliana live in Indiana after getting a Vermont civil union. The relationship lasts 11 years. When it breaks up they don't bother taking care of the legal bits. Lilly moves on to California and 5 years pass.

Liliana is now in a new relationship with Susan and they want to get a California domestic partnership. But they can't because Lilly is still unionized to Juliana. So off she goes to a California court seeking termination of her Vermont civil union.

Juliana, who accumulated considerable assets since the split, finds herself getting deunionized in a community property state almost 2,000 miles away. Not to mention that in California it only takes 10 years to be considered a long marriage. Since Indiana still has no civil union law she has little choice but to fight for her jewelry in the California sunshine.

The same kind of story could be told about a traditional marriage. Once the required residency is established a Vermont marriage can be terminated in any state. But normally people get divorced in the state where they live. Judges don't like people who shop around from state to state looking for the most favorable divorce laws.

What makes the Julianna/Liliana story different is simply that it's more likely to occur. Civil union partners are inclined to delay getting legally terminated. It's just too difficult to move to Vermont for such a long period. Also, as other states pass civil union or same sex marriage laws their courts will probably accept a "shopping" approach as long as the state where the partners live doesn't yet have such laws.

The Last Word on Civil Unions

Nothing in this chapter is meant to discourage anyone from entering into a civil union. Just don't jump in without thinking. Like a traditional marriage a civil union is a complex legal relationship. The difference is that relevant laws outside of Vermont for the most part do not exist. Where they do exist, how such laws are interpreted by the courts will continue to develop for some time to come.

Yeah, but love makes everyone blind to all this stuff and many will just close their eyes and hope for the best. That may not be the wisest approach.

Special Note: *At the time this current edition of Divorce in Vermont was published Vermont, California, Massachusetts, and Connecticut were the only states to allow some form of civil union or same sex marriage A few other states also appear on the verge of implementing same sex partnership law. This doesn't necessarily reduce the risks discussed in this chapter. The situation remains similar to buying a house next to a vacant lot. You never can be sure what is going to be built on it.*

Many civil union benefits remain unclear and may be limited for most people. A key step forward will be when the federal government recognizes these relationships for tax and other purposes. That event is still thought to be several years away. Meanwhile, consider using additional means to achieve the desired results. That includes having well thought out wills, living wills, pre and/or post civil union agreements, establishing both parties as legal parents, etc.

CHAPTER 13

Determining Income

Why Income Is So Important

When it comes to settling the financial issues of divorce nothing is more important than the family income. Love, spite, kids, support and everything else only get taken care of to the extent there is money to do so. Sure, the judge or magistrate can sometimes offset low earnings by manipulating the property distribution. But families with little income usually have few assets. If there are any, it's most likely a house and a car. Things they can't sell because they need them.

Vermont provides welfare and similar help for those with low incomes while the rich have few financial problems. However, the majority caught in the middle are left to cut back on everything until the bleeding stops. Yet there may be more money than you think. Vermont looks well beyond the tax records and makes judgments based on what each party could be earning, should be earning, or is earning but not reporting.

Checking Out the W-2

While the amount indicated on a spouse's most recent income tax form represents a starting point, it isn't necessarily the final figure used by the court. For example, what if the husband was laid off during the year for several months, but is now back at work? If the judge or magistrate relied only on his latest reported income it would look pretty low. The reverse is also true. Perhaps the husband is in real estate sales and it's been an unusually profitable period. In order to be fair his earning performance over the longer term should be considered and not just the most recent year.

Therefore, a person's earning history for three, four or even five years including overtime and bonuses is used to find an average income. Using this data, the judge often gains a good idea of what each party's future income is likely to be.

But sometimes the past doesn't predict the future. Let's say a wife recently got a big promotion or a new job with a huge pay increase. Maybe she just finished law school and is unemployed, but interviewing for a position. Now the court has to look forward to determine the right income to use. What kind of salary, overtime and bonus is the new posting likely to pay? There are plenty of statistics available to make a good estimate.

Besides salary, income includes earnings from rental property, bank deposits, mutual funds, stocks and bonds, etc. The same goes for money received through pensions and annuities.

Working "Off the Books" and Other Misadventures

Income that's paid off the books is also considered part of an individual's earnings. This could be money made weekends clearing and splitting trees, or by selling hand-knitted sweaters at the town market, or from grade "A" dark amber maple syrup sold out the back of the barn.

The judge and magistrate will want to include all cash income as well. In this case the term "cash" is a substitute for the words "earnings that I don't report to the IRS." This is particularly popular with some handymen and other private businesses. Frequently a person has more unreported income than reported earnings. And don't forget about undisclosed tips.

Non-cash transactions are also considered to be income in Vermont. For example, a farm hand in Springfield who gets free housing as part of his job will have the rental value of the accommodations plus the cost of heating and electricity added to his earnings. The same goes for the personal use of a company car that a sales-man or executive might receive.

And barter payments get counted too. In these transactions someone does something like paint a house in exchange for being given an almost new snowmobile. One-time events won't mean much to the court, but there are people who conduct a large part of their working activities using barter.

The Spy Who Loved You

Go to court thinking you can hide this extra income and you'll most likely be disappointed. Remember, your spouse knows you like a book and his or her attorney has seen it all before. So guess who's going to spill the beans?

To help things along, each spouse has the right to receive copies of the other's tax reports and business records. It's important that these documents provide an accurate earnings picture. Judges and magistrates take an immediate dislike to anyone presenting false or misleading information.

Everything Is Not Enough

Even if a party is totally honest it may not be good enough. When a person chooses to take a lower paying job it's called being "voluntarily under-employed." A common example is a self-employed professional or craftsman who earns less than if he or she were doing the same job for a corporation or general contractor. Another example is when a previously well compensated executive decides to drop out and take up a lower income producing activity like landscape painting.

In these situations the court first determines if it's likely these higher paying jobs are actually available. If they are then the court will assume the higher income level when doing their calculations (referred to as imputed income). The judge or magistrate can't force the easygoing spouse to take the better paid position, but the amount of child support and alimony specified in the final order may leave little choice.

The classic under-employed spouse is the stay at home mom or dad. Once the kids are of school age Vermont courts generally assume that the stay at home spouse is choosing not to work.

Therefore, an income for that spouse will be imputed by the court. The amount of assumed earnings is based on the spouse's previous work history, any special training or skills he or she has and the local job market.

The court is always optimistic. It believes that almost everyone is employable. So unless there is a limiting medical problem or an issue of an equally serious nature, like having to care for a chronically ill child, it's pretty hard for the stay at home to avoid getting assigned some amount of income.

And Still More Money

One profitable area for the other party's lawyer is the self employed spouse who earns a mere $8,000 a year, yet magically affords a Corvette, a golf club membership, a large house in Shelburne and a four bedroom "cabin" with a view at Stowe. It's easy to impute a salary based on this miracle worker being employed by a local corporation with a salary well beyond $8,000.

It's even more profitable to rework the business's income statement in a way that shows how the poorly paid owner is really making $200,000 a year, and based on this actual income the business is worth $2 million instead of the claimed value of $100,000. The moral is to be realistic about any business earnings from the start. Don't wait for the opposing attorney to destroy your credibility in front of the court.

And finally, on a less obvious note, the state has a formula for considering the appreciation of non-income producing assets. This includes such investments as undeveloped land, artwork, antiques and car collections. If those items are significantly going up in value, then that annual increase may be added in as part of one or both spouses' income.

Making Cents from the Dollars

By now you realize that the income calculations for divorce purposes can be quite different from those used by the tax authorities. How much gets reported as earnings or even what is actually earned is not always the measure of total income. The court's definition of income is a person's ability to contribute to the support of the children and/or former spouse. The IRS may have a different one, but that is not important.

If either party can change his or her needs or ability to pay by doing something else, then the court will assign income based on that assumption. The fact that a spouse plans to study French literature instead of continuing to captain a 747 airliner is of no consideration to a Vermont judge. The state's point of view is that he or she should have thought of that before entering into matrimony/parenthood.

A Friend in Need

Many people believe the court assumes that a non-related adult living with one of the divorcing parties (referred to as "cohabitation") is sharing the housing costs and other living expenses. They also believe that because of this "extra" income the judge will make adjustments in the amount of spousal support being paid or received depending on which party has the additional income. This isn't correct.

Vermont's Supreme Court in a close 3 to 2 decision determined that such extra income (whether actually paid or not) shouldn't be considered when seeking to modify spousal support. Nor is it likely to be a factor in establishing the original alimony order.

For example, a divorcing mother and her son live in their Essex marital home with Patricia, a non-related adult. The court will not take into account the money that Patty is paying to cover her portion of the household expenses when deciding how much support the mother requires.

The reverse of the above situation is also true. If the spouse paying support is cohabitating with either a lover or a friend the court won't consider household support payments (and certainly not a lover's salary) when determining the paying party's ability to provide alimony.

Keep in mind we are not talking about income earned by renting an apartment in a party's house. That's business income and will be considered.

Also, if the spouse receiving alimony gets married the new spouse's income may (not always) open the door to having the maintenance modified. But if the paying spouse gets married it's not a reason for the court to either increase or a decrease the payments.

The Final Twist

Spousal support is income to the person who gets it. So the magistrate will add the alimony payment to the receiving spouse's income before doing the child support calculation. At the same time, alimony gets subtracted from the income of the paying party before making the same calculation.

CHAPTER 14

Divorce Strategies and Issues

It Takes Two to Tangle

A strong message runs throughout this book. A fair-minded couple with the assistance, as required, of lawyers, mediators, accountants, appraisers, child agencies, etc. is in the best position to reach a satisfactory conclusion.

Destructive behavior is destined to send the emotional life of the family members down the toilet right along with their finances. Yet, even when both sides understand the danger, many get run over by this locomotive. Each spouse feels the other is being unreasonable. That "other spouse" refuses to be realistic. His or her ideas are simply "nuts." "How could anyone think that way?"

A True Story About Japan and Baseball

This is a good time to tell a true sports story.

Several years ago an American athlete was playing baseball for a Japanese team when his son became gravely ill.

Brain surgery was required with his survival uncertain. So the American player immediately flew to the U.S. to be there for the operation. That's when all hell broke loose.

His Japanese teammates, the Japanese media and the average citizen of Japan were completely outraged. It was beyond their comprehension how such a valuable player could leave the team in the middle of the season. One Japanese player exclaimed, "If my mother was on her deathbed, I would never leave the team."

The reaction in the United States was just the opposite. No one understood the apparently heartless attitude of the Japanese. After all, the man's son was close to death. It seemed the Japanese don't love their families as we do in America. There could be no other reasonable explanation.

Let's stop the story for a moment. Does any of this remind you of talking to your spouse? Two sides miles apart and each positive the other is completely wrong. Is there really only one reasonable way of looking at things? Now, back to the story.

As Americans we believe that the right thing to do in this situation was obvious, so how did the Japanese explain their feelings? Well, it was obvious to them as well.

A Japanese ballplayer knows his family loves him. But his teammates don't love him the way his family does. The other players would never forgive him if he left. So, it's his family's love that allows a Japanese player to maintain his obligation to the team.

Clearly, a huge cultural issue was at work here. However, the story makes an important point. There is more than one way of looking at virtually any situation.

It's possible for two honorable people to disagree and for both of them to be right based on their legitimate needs and motivations.

If you feel your spouse is being unreasonable, try to see the situation from his or her point of view. Don't let these differences prevent the two of you from finding a meaningful resolution. Remember, men are from Mars and women are from Venus.

Also, keep in mind the consequences of not working out an agreement. Then everything gets left up to the lawyers and the judges. God only knows what planets they're all from!

The Evil Doer

But sometimes if it walks like a duck, and talks like a duck, it's a duck. There are spouses with less than honorable intentions. A weaker spouse may see divorce as an opportunity to establish an early retirement nest egg. Or perhaps just the opposite is true. The spouse with the great job and the greater prospects wants to shed his or her responsibilities towards the more dependent partner.

Too often the good spouse believes that by being reasonable the other side will be reasonable too. So he or she makes a decent offer which the evil spouse rejects out of hand. Then, without the evil doer making a counter proposal the good spouse sends an even more attractive revision. That is also quickly rejected.

If the evil one does make a proposal it's usually so outrageous that it has no meaning. Still believing that a compromise is possible the good spouse faxes back counter proposals to these preposterous solutions where they disappear into the vacuum of the evil doer's cold, cold heart. A one-sided negotiation is a fool's game.

Sometimes the situation is as clear as the one described above. Often it's more subtle. One party is providing fair offers and the other side is discussing them and suggesting alternatives. It looks like progress is being made. However, the other side puts nothing in writing. Any proposal not in writing is less than worthless. Consider the cost of such wasted negotiations if mediators and lawyers get involved. Refuse to be manipulated in such a manner.

A Lesson in the Art of War

In war the most important objective is to control the time and place of the battle.

If after reading the Japanese baseball story you still believe that your spouse is up to no good in the negotiation, then run (do not walk) to a lawyer and demand that you move through the divorce process as fast as possible.

Getting the court date set sends a strong message. You're saying "either negotiate with me now in good faith or do it in court (the place of battle) on such and such date (the time of the battle)."

Have you seen how ferociously a junkyard dog defends the junkyard? Take that mongrel out of its familiar territory and watch it hurriedly walk along, head down and tail between its legs. At the junkyard, the dog would bite your head off. On the street it goes out of its way to avoid passing near you.

Many spouses who are tough guys or gals when going up against their marriage partner at home become weak lambs or act like fools in front of the judge. This is not their territory. Their power to manipulate is gone. By forcing the time and the place you are now the manipulator. You're taking charge.

If the problem spouse is smart he or she will get down to serious negotiation before the trial. If you have a dumb one on your hands, well, there's nothing much you can do about it. Go to court. The judge will give you a better deal than any your "better half" has in mind.

Remember that the difference between threatening to set a court date and setting one is night and day. Maintaining a false hope that the other spouse will see the light is far worse than having no hope. SET THE COURT DATE!

Sometimes Things Are Too Comfortable

Another recommendation of this book is to err on the side of generosity when agreeing to temporary payments. However, it shouldn't be done blindly. If there is any doubt about the cooperative attitude of the other party, then try to keep these temporary amounts in line with what is likely to be in the final order.

That's because an excessively favorable deal made at the CMSC or imposed by the judge and the magistrate in temporary orders can kill the receiving spouse's incentive to push things towards a final resolution. In fact, the comfortable spouse often works to slow things down.

This can be done in many imaginative ways. The first is for the delaying party to stretch out the negotiations by always making success appear to be just around the corner. When the other party catches on to this game the comfortable spouse may suddenly demand additional or revised data. For example, he or she now wants the appraisals redone because too much time has passed even though it's unlikely the values have changed. Not surprisingly, the appraiser is backlogged for several weeks.

Another way to extend the process is by requesting a substantial amount of court time to present the case. If one of the parties demands a day and a half trial it's certain to set things back several months while everyone waits for a large space in the court calendar to become available. He or she may get "sick" on the day of the trial or change lawyers just before the big event.

The judge will eventually realize what's going on and put a foot down, but initially the benefit of the doubt is given. Meanwhile, six months, a year, or even more can go by.

And Sometimes It Is the Lawyer

Not all lawyers are helpful. While the large majority work to resolve issues in a fair and equitable manner, some may lead their clients astray. Attorneys who put "stars" in the eyes of their clients by making them believe that they can "have it all," do everyone a disservice.

The demanding party becomes certain that the other spouse should be giving more or getting less depending on the situation. Why? Because his or her lawyer says so.

The cost of maintaining an unrealistic attitude is easily measured by counting the extra billing hours of all the lawyers and other professionals that will be forced to get involved. The emotional price is high as well. Make certain your attorney knows you want a realistic appraisal of the situation.

Who's Paying for It All?

The temporary order may require the high income spouse to pay the legal bills for both sides. This makes sense if the other party has no separate financial resources. However, the poorer spouse will sometimes take advantage of this situation and go off on a legal spending spree. In addition to the excess cost, a party's ability to delay the process gains a significant advantage if the attorney fees can be ignored in the short term.

Indeed, the payment is coming from the couple's joint income, but the unpaying spouse doesn't actually see the money being spent. It's like shopping with a credit card.

So, it's better to have anticipated legal expenses budgeted into the poor spouse's monthly support payment while the divorce is in process. This provides some control over the amount of legal activities undertaken. It also keeps the parties in personal touch with how much is being spent.

If such an abuse is taking place the paying spouse needs to have the plug pulled. While judges don't like to revise temporary orders they will do so if the abuse is clear. The reverse of this is also true. A spouse receiving a small legal budget as part of the support payment can seek an increase if the actions of the other party generate extraordinary legal costs.

Patience Is a Virtue

In a cooperative divorce the overall system works pretty well. But if one party decides to disrupt the process then it will move at a snail's pace.

Most people react poorly to delay. As things drag on frustration increases. This lowers expectations and weakens the resolve necessary to get an equitable settlement. The frustrated spouse is often put in an impossible financial and emotional position.

There is no simple solution to this headache. If you live and breathe your divorce 24 hours a day any slowdown will feel two or three times longer than the actual delay. Do the best you can with your attorney's help to stabilize the situation. Then find an activity to take some of your attention away from the misery.

Try learning a new language, take up tennis, plant a garden or volunteer at a nursing home (nursing homes have a way of putting your problems in perspective!). Don't ignore the divorce process. That's a good way of losing control. But over-controlling it can have a similar result. Patience is a certainly a virtue during times like these.

Use Only In Case of Emergency

Sometimes things can't wait. Sometimes the situation is not only frustrating, but really dangerous. Negotiating a resolution is not a choice. It's time for a different strategy. By implementing a relief from abuse order things will move at warp speed (faster than supersonic).

It starts when a fearful spouse signs a Family Court affidavit stating that he or she and/or the children have been physically abused or are in imminent danger of being injured by the other spouse. A temporary order requiring the dangerous party to leave the house is immediately issued. In addition, the order specifies that the fearful spouse, at least until the hearing, has custody of the children and sole use of the family house. All this is done without a hearing or the other spouse being present.

Notification to the dangerous party is made within three days (sometimes in a few hours). Twenty minutes after notification the subject of the order must be out of the house with the police managing the departure.

Not more than ten days following the order date the case gets before the judge. By this time the accused spouse is already out of the house. If the judge finds in favor of the complaining spouse the court will issue a final relief from abuse order.

The final order usually grants the complaining spouse custody of the children and use of the family home. In a few cases it may also assign up to three months of support payments to be paid by the abusing spouse for the children and the complaining spouse (only if the couple were living together).

But judges don't want a relief from abuse order to be a substitute for a divorce. The focus is on securing the safety of the complaining spouse and children. Therefore, support payments, the division of assets, etc. are determined at the temporary hearing and child support hearing if there is a subsequent filing for divorce, legal separation, or child support (see the chapter on Vermont's divorce process). Remember, under a relief from abuse order the parties remain married.

Most importantly the abusing spouse will have severe limits placed on his or her ability to contact the complaining spouse and the children. Visitation may be supervised or out of the question depending on the type of abuse. Violation of these restrictions is a criminal act and often results in arrest and prosecution.

Vermont law requires that the final relief from abuse order be for a specified period of time. Most are for one or two years, though some last longer. The court can be asked to renew it if the issue is not resolved by the expiration date.

Finally, if someone is unfairly accused of abuse it's very important that he or she fights and wins the case at the final abuse hearing. Once a spouse is found culpable and removed from the family it's extremely difficult to regain the rights lost under the order.

Children Should Be Off Limits

Even wars have rules. During the divorce process a good rule is to keep the children out of the argument. Unfortunately, this does not always hold true. One parent may attempt to turn the children against the other. Perhaps it's just spite or to enhance a negotiating position. Maybe he or she believes it's a way to gain custody. These strategies usually backfire with the results becoming the exact opposite of what was intended.

If a spouse is using the children to manipulate the situation, action needs to be taken at once. Depending on how serious things become, it's possible to get an emergency hearing. In extreme cases, the judge can restrict either visitation or custodial rights depending on who's at fault. The court takes a dim view of a parent who sets a child against the other parent. Remember, one of the criteria for obtaining physical custody is the custodial parent's desire and ability to foster a positive relationship with the other parent.

The Ultimate Tactic

Please remember, the ideal strategy is to have both sides working together towards a fair settlement.

CHAPTER 15

The Perils of Living Together

Life in the Fast Lane

Any influence the Puritan colonies had on the Green Mountain State's character disappeared long ago. We talk longingly about the sleepy old ways, but the fact is that Vermont sets the pace for non-traditional lifestyles. This seems particularly true when it comes to cohabitation. Many couples living together never bother to get married. Together they buy cars, take out loans, have lots of children and even own a house, but they never take the time to get hitched.

In a state that invented civil unions and where hippies almost took over the government in the 1960's one might think common law marriages would be common. Not so! Somehow this one missed the legislative boat. There is no common law marriage in Vermont. A guy and gal can share room and board for 50 years and they are still not legally married until they say officially "I do."

So what happens when Rosie and Phil, a Hardwick couple that has lived together for 15 years, decide to break up? Just as with divorcing spouses, the best approach is for them to work out an acceptable settlement on their own. One thing neither can do is file a complaint with the Family Court. Complaints are for married customers only.

In fact, none of the alimony and property distribution laws that protect married partners apply to live-together couples. Unlike in long marriages, and even in some short ones, neither Phil nor Rosie is obligated to support the other now or in the future. And their property settlement will be decided by the Superior Court where the equitable distribution laws don't apply.

That's because live-together relationships are viewed as partnerships, not much different than the accounting firm down the street. The one big difference is that the accountants have a partnership agreement that spells out the rights of the parties. You can bet your snowmobile that Phil and Rosie have very little in writing.

Living Together with the Kids

The Family Court is responsible for dealing with the children of a live-together couple that is breaking up. In general, things involving these kids work the same as in the divorce process. This is all reviewed in the Paternity and the Status of Children chapter. Related issues can be found in the chapters covering child custody, visitation and support. Grandparents can also review the chapter on grandparental rights.

Lee Marvin Should Have Lived in Vermont

Some time ago actor Lee Marvin made the term palimony famous. Lee lived with a woman for many years who claimed to have given up her career to keep the home fires burning. Eventually they split and Lee was sued for palimony.

Palimony is essentially alimony paid to one live-together partner by the other after they go their separate ways. The logic is that a long term commitment has been established just as in a long marriage. While there have been some large palimony awards, Mr. Marvin basically won this high profile case when the woman was granted a trivial support payment. Later on she ended up with Dick Van Dyke, but that's a different story.

Back in Hardwick, Phil is also looking forward to collecting some palimony. It seems that Rosie was the ambitious partner and started a successful Vermont cuisine restaurant called the Woodchuck Upchuck. Phil, meanwhile, wasn't employed, preferring to take care of the home and the children. He speaks of sacrificing his personal career for Rosie's Upchuck success. He also claims to have contributed half the money to start the business. Now, as the profits roll in he feels entitled to some kind of maintenance payment following the break-up.

If Phil was married to Rosie for those 15 years he might have gotten his meal ticket punched. After all, it would have been a long marriage and in divorces the judge takes into account the sacrifices one spouse made in support of the other. But in this case they were only living together. There is no palimony in Vermont.

Still, Phil has one slim hope. In this case Phil was the primary caregiver and will likely get the children. The court sometimes awards a maintenance supplement payment to the custodial parent. Its purpose is to assist in the support of the children by giving the custodial parent enough money to provide a proper home, etc. The supplement is likely to be smaller than a normal spousal maintenance payment and it lasts only while the kids are eligible for child support. Phil's disappointed.

What's Yours Is Yours and Mine Is Mine

Phil's biggest surprise comes when he discovers how the assets will be divided. Equitable distribution, where the judge evaluates the needs of both parties and allocates property like some kind of state sponsored Robin Hood, is only for divorcing couples. When a live-together situation breaks up the process for handing out the assets is referred to as a civil partition.

Since Phil supplied half the initial $50,000 Upchuck investment he went to court demanding 50% of the business' current $350,000 value. In such a case the first thing the court does is review the partnership agreement which, for a live-together couple, is similar to a pre- or post-nuptial agreement. If there is no written document the judge will then look at who owns what.

You will recall that when ending a long marriage it doesn't matter too much who owns what. Generally, it all gets put into the same shared pot. Even in a short marriage joint ownership is often assumed for property acquired during the marriage. This is not the case in a live-together property settlement (civil partition). Therefore, it's important whose name is on an account, deed, loan, registration, etc.

All the documents related to the Woodchuck Upchuck restaurant are only in Rosie's name. That includes the deed for the building, the bills for its furnishings and the bank accounts. There is no written business or live-together agreement between Rosie and Phil. The only item with Phil's name on it is his check to Rosie for $25,000 covering half the startup costs. Importantly, Phil never did any work directly for the restaurant.

In the end, the court could possibly decide that Phil is not a half owner of the restaurant, but rather just a creditor. He doesn't get $175,000 (half of the $350,000 appraised value). Instead, the judge orders Rosie to repay Phil the $25,000 he "loaned" her along with interest. Rosie keeps the $350,000 asset and Phil's really unhappy.

Becoming an "Honest" Man and Woman

What happens when a live-together couple eventually gets married and then divorced? In determining whether it was a long or short marriage is any credit given for the time they lived together before the marriage? The short answer is "maybe yes and maybe no."

Vermont courts recognize that it's not unreasonable to include the live-together time when determining the length of a marriage. The main question is whether or not the couple when living together acted like a married couple. Did they have joint bank accounts, share expenses, etc? Counting this live-together time is still new for Vermont and a lot depends on the specific judge hearing the case.

Nevertheless, getting married has several important impacts. The most important is that all the issues are now decided by the Family Court. That's a big difference.

Assume that the Woodchuck Upchuck was started while Phil and Rosie were living together. Later on they got married and the marriage lasted 15 years, or the court included some live-together time which resulted in a combined total of at least 15 years.

Phil is part of a long marriage. The court is likely to consider the restaurant a marital asset even though it was started when they were living together and everything is in Rosie's name. Phil supported her by taking care of the kids and the house while she cooked her way to fame and fortune. In the eyes of Vermont, Upchuck's success was a joint effort.

Also, the judge realizes that Phil is unlikely to ever achieve a high paying career, while Rosie is in a position to continue making a substantial income after the divorce. So, Phil might get 50% of the restaurant and alimony, or more of the restaurant and less or no alimony, or some other variation on that theme. After all, he is nearing retirement age and will need an asset and/or income base to help him live. Phil is finally happy.

If the combined live-together and married years resulted in only a short marriage, Phil would have gotten less. But, depending on how short it was he might still receive a share of the restaurant or possibly enough alimony to transition him to an independent life.

The key factor is that at some point Phil and Rosie got married. If they were not married when they broke up there could be no equitable distribution.

What Does All This Have to Do With You?

Some readers may wonder why a chapter on living together is in a book about divorce. They are in the minority. The majority knows why.

While there are no official statistics, it's clear that many spouses are into their next relationship well before the divorce is granted. After the final order, newly divorced parties often prefer not to rush into marriage again. They'd rather come and go as they please.

But that doesn't mean there aren't risks. The stay at home mom or dad in a live-together situation who ignores these risks is in for a big surprise if it all comes crashing down. No job, no alimony, no pension sharing, maybe not even the house or car if these things are only in the other partner's name. Pretty much not much at all. The working partner is taking a risk too.

Divorce involves the family and the Family Court is very sensitive to family issues. Breaking up a live-together couple is a different story. The Superior Court lacks much of the care and concern found in the Family Court's process. It becomes more like dissolving a business deal.

So, live-together relationships need to be run like a business.

- Keep assets in the name of the party who owns them.

- Keep loans in the name of the party who benefits from them.

- Joint assets should be in both parties' names.

- Have a written agreement that clearly outlines how joint properties and loans will be divided if the relationship ends.

- If you are staying home to care for the children while the other party works, put a support plan in writing that gets implemented if things fall apart.

Oh, and have a nice life.

Appendix

Summary of Vermont's Divorce Process
(shown in the usual order of occurrence)

Complaint—One party prepares a complaint (infrequently both parties will do this). If a lawyer is involved the attorney prepares the complaint and it is sent to the other spouse. If there is no attorney then the spouse initiating the complaint can prepare the document provided by the court.

Notice—Sent to the non-complaining spouse by either the complaining spouse's attorney or directly by the court. The notice includes a copy of the complaint. The non-complaining spouse is expected to sign an acknowledgement or return receipt to demonstrate to the court that they received notification that the divorce has been filed. The acknowledgement only indicates that the complaint was received, but does not signify any agreement or disagreement with the contents of the complaint. If there is a problem in delivering the notice to the non-complaining spouse a sheriff can be used to deliver it or the notice can be printed in a local paper for three weeks.

Filing—The complaint is filed once the court receives the complaint. If the complaining party is using a lawyer the filing date will usually be when the non-complaining spouse returns the acknowledgement for filing with the complaint or when the complaint is filed with a request that the court serve the notice to the non-complaining spouse by registered mail. However, if no lawyer is involved and the spouse draws up the complaint at the Family Court's office it can be filed at that time and then served by the court.

Interim Order—This order is automatically issued by the court once it receives the complaint. If a lawyer is involved this will happen after filing is complete. The interim order prohibits either party from relocating the children out of the state and making major changes to assets, debts, and other key marriage issues.

Pro Se Class—A one hour class for a pro se litigant (a party not using a lawyer). It provides an overview of the entire divorce process. (Mandatory in most Family Court districts.)

Case Managers Status Conference (CMSC)—A meeting between spouses (including lawyers if used) and a court clerk to collect agreed stipulations (any terms the parties have agreed to). If parental rights and responsibilities, parent-child contact and spousal support are agreed to at the CMSC then there is no need for temporary hearings to decide these issues. If all divorce issues are permanently resolved at the CMSC then final stipulations are sent to the magistrate and judge to prepare the final order and the child support order (there are no temporary hearings and only a brief final hearing which under certain conditions can be avoided as well).

COPE Class—Mandatory four hour class for couples with minor children. Parents are taught how to help their children cope with the changes and stress of divorce.

Temporary Hearing—The judge makes the following temporary decisions: child custody, child visitation, alimony, division of selected assets (home, auto), responsibility to service major debt (mortgage, car loan, etc.). The temporary hearing can be held before the CMSC if there is an urgent need (hardship due to interim orders, need for a restraining order, etc.). There is no temporary hearing if the parties agree to these issues prior to or at the CMSC.

Temporary Order—Specifies the judge's decisions from the temporary hearing.

Initial Child Support Hearing—The magistrate determines child support which may result in a temporary or final order. He or she might also set temporary alimony if the judge allows and approve other temporary agreements such as child custody/visitation rights, etc.. already agreed to at the CMSC. This avoids having a temporary hearing.

Initial Child Support Order—Specifies the magistrate's determination or it can be the magistrate's acceptance of the parties' stipulated agreement. This order is final (except for a change in circumstances) unless the parties have requested that it be temporary.

Status Conference (SC)—Informal meeting with the judge in order to try and settle issues the parties are unable to resolve and to plan for the disposition of the case. The judge may provide advice and an indication of the court's approach to the issues involved. Such guidance from the court is intended to assist the parties in finding solutions to resolve the case.

Motion Hearing—In these hearings the court will address issues the parties cannot settle between themselves and require the court's help in a specific written document specifying the issue, and the relief sought. Unlike the SC, the judge issues an order which is binding on the parties until the final order.

Second CMSC—Usually held just before the final hearing. Its purpose is to find out if the parties have reached agreement on additional issues. If all issues have been settled then stipulations will be drawn up and forwarded to the judge and/or magistrate for review and approval. If only some items have been agreed to the final hearing will focus on undecided issues.

Final Hearing—The final hearing is a trial. The judge determines all the outstanding issues of the divorce with the exception of child support. However, if the judge feels that based on the outcome of the other divorce issues (alimony, child custody/visitation, etc.) a review of the child support order is required, a second child support hearing will be held.

Final Child Support Hearing—If the judge determines during the final hearing that a review of child support is required, a second child support hearing will be held. However, if the judge feels that no child support changes are needed the initial child support order will automatically become final. Keep in mind that child support is never really final. The court can be asked to revise it any time there are substantial changes in financial needs and/or financial resources.

Final Child Support Order—If no child support review is suggested by the judge after the final hearing, the initial child support order will become final. If a review is suggested by the judge, the magistrate will issue a final child support order following a final child support hearing.

Final Order—The ultimate decree or document which itemizes all the final provisions pertaining to the children, division of assets and debts, and spousal maintenance. The decree may be based upon the parties' agreement; or in the event the parties cannot reach an agreement, the decree will be the decision of the judge after hearing evidence from both parties.

Nisi Period—Lasts for 90 days after the final order is issued. During this time errors in the final order can be revised. It is also possible for the parties to mutually agree to have the divorce rescinded. If both parties agree, and with the court's approval, the nisi period can be can be reduced or omitted.

Divorce Is Absolute—At the end of the nisi period the divorce automatically becomes absolute. Only at this point are the parties legally divorced.

Diagram of Vermont's Divorce Process

Note: The below chart gives a general outline of the sequence of events. However, depending on the specific situation, the process can vary.

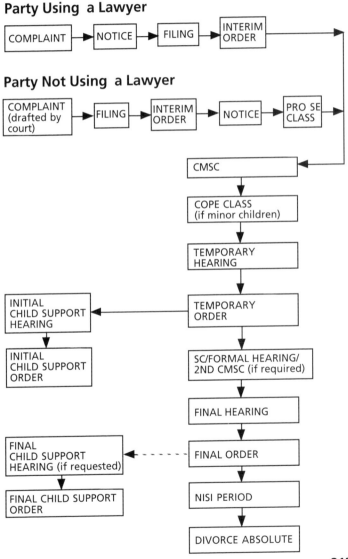

Party Using a Lawyer

COMPLAINT → NOTICE → FILING → INTERIM ORDER →

Party Not Using a Lawyer

COMPLAINT (drafted by court) → FILING → INTERIM ORDER → NOTICE → PRO SE CLASS →

CMSC

COPE CLASS (if minor children)

TEMPORARY HEARING

INITIAL CHILD SUPPORT HEARING ← TEMPORARY ORDER

INITIAL CHILD SUPPORT ORDER

SC/FORMAL HEARING/ 2ND CMSC (if required)

FINAL HEARING

FINAL CHILD SUPPORT HEARING (if requested) ← FINAL ORDER

FINAL CHILD SUPPORT ORDER

NISI PERIOD

DIVORCE ABSOLUTE

Things to Bring to the First Meeting with a Lawyer

A. A List of Questions You Have Regarding Your Divorce and the Divorce Process

B. Income Information
1. Tax returns and all IRS forms related to the returns (joint and separate) for at least 3 years
2. Private business tax returns (if any) for at least 3 years
3. Pay stubs for both spouses for last four months

C. Property Information
1. Real estate owned
   - mortgages and notes
   - names of owners
   - deeds
   - assessment notices
   - lister's card
   - closing statements
   - source of down payments and purchase prices
   - appraisal reports
2. Vehicles owned (cars, tractors, 4-wheelers, boats, snowmobiles)
   - year, make and model
   - debt, monthly payments, creditor
   - blue book value
3. Bank accounts and stocks and bonds
   - statements showing value
   - date of purchase and source of funds
4. Pensions, 401(k)/Keogh plans, etc.
   - plan description
   - statements showing valuation
5. Life insurance policies (especially those with cash value)
   - statement showing value
6. Other significant assets (art collections, sports memorabilia, antiques, time share, royalties, patents, etc.)
   - description and value of each asset (appraisal reports)
   - location of the assets
   - date of purchase and source of funds

D. Other Debts
1. Credit card debt

- credit card numbers
- account ownership (joint or separate)
- list of items charged
- debt owed (current statement)
2. Installment debt/student loans
   - name of debtor
   - purpose of debt
   - amount and terms

E. Family Information
1. Marriage information
   - names and date of births of the spouses
   - date started living together (if you lived together before the marriage)
   - date of marriage
   - date of separation
   - pre-nuptial agreements (agreements made before the marriage)
   - post-nuptial agreements (agreements made during the marriage)
   - separation agreements, mediation agreements
   - outline of any other arrangements (written or not written) regarding the separation such as support payments, child support, etc.
   - medical information
     —special requirements and conditions
     —medical/dental insurance source and cost
2. Children information
   - names, date of births
   - school issues
     —name and address of schools
     —teachers' names
     —grade and general performance
   - special activities (religion, camps, sports, music, etc.)
   - special needs (medical/medication, tutors, braces, etc.)
   - pediatrician's name/address (include any other regularly seen doctors)
   - daycare provider
     —name/address
     —weekly and annual cost
3. Other legal documents
   - prior divorces of either spouse
     —divorce dates and copies of the decrees

- other court documents regarding issues of family abuse or criminal activity
- probate papers, guardianships, trusts
- any significant lawsuits, worker's compensation claims
- Social Security status and payments if any received by either spouse

4. Marriage time line
   - Create an outline of all important marriage events starting with the marriage itself and continuing on in the order they occurred right up until the present day. If the parties lived together for a long period of time it is useful to start from the time of living together. Things listed in this time line will include the marriage date, employment and related changes (promotions, salary increases, unemployment periods), legal events, birth of children, reallocations, serious medical events, the separation, etc.

5. Typical family life
   - give a brief description of typical life of the family (use actual events for examples)
     —school day
     —weekend
     —vacation

Things to Do After the Divorce

A. Get a certified copy of the divorce.

B. Retrieve important original documents given to the lawyers during the divorce.
   1. deeds
   2. tax documents and pay stubs
   3. photos

C. Change all loans, mortgages and credit cards to the name of the party that is responsible for the debt. If the names cannot be removed at the time of the divorce, followup every six months to see if the situation has changed.

D. Record deeds in the name of the party who owns the property.

E. Change the names on relevant insurance policies (auto, home, etc.).

F. Change the beneficiary on life insurance, pensions, 401(k)/Keogh plans.

G. Provide proper notification of a Qualified Domestic Relationship Order (QDRO) to the pension plan administrator if appropriate.

H. Notify your health insurance company of the reduction in family members covered or, if you were covered by your spouse's policy, secure alternative insurance. (Vermont consumer assistance provides information on obtaining health insurance at 1-800-631-7788.)

I. Alter your will to reflect the changes brought on by the divorce.

J. Change the names on automobile registrations and titles.

K. If it was a high conflict case, maintain a confidential journal of the children's visits, activities, and other significant events.

L. Each year obtain a copy of your ex-spouse's tax return and pay stubs. The end of May is the best time to obtain this information which must be provided under Vermont law.

M. File a modification with the court when the last minor

child reaches 18 years old or graduates from high school (whichever comes last) to get a release from employer withholding of child support.

N. Register the divorce with the proper agencies if you move to another state.

Vermont Family Courts

Location	Telephone/Fax*
Addison Family Court 7 Mahady Court Middlebury VT 05753	Tel: 388-4605 Fax: 388-4643
Bennington Family Court 200 Veterans Memorial Dr Bennington VT 05201	Tel: 447-2729 Fax: 447-2794
Caledonia Family Court 1126 Main St, Ste 1 St Johnsbury VT 05819	Tel: 748-6600 Fax: 748-6603
Chittenden Family Court 32 Cherry St, Suite 300 Burlington VT 05401	Tel: 651-1800 Fax: 651-1740
Essex Family Court PO Box 75 Guildhall VT 05905	Tel: 676-3910 Fax: 676-3463
Franklin Family Court 36 Lake St St Albans VT 05478	Tel: 524-7997 Fax: 524-7946
Grand Isle Family Court Grand Isle Courthouse North Hero VT 05474	Tel: 372-8350 Fax: 372-3221
Lamoille Family Court PO Box 489 Hyde Park VT 05655	Tel: 888-3887 Fax: 888-2591
Orange Family Court	Tel: 685-4610

Orange County Courthouse   Fax: 685-3246
5 Court St
Chelsea VT 05038

Orleans Family Court   Tel: 334-3305
247 Main St, Suite 1   Fax: 334-3385
Newport VT 05855

Rutland Family Court   Tel: 786-5856
83 Center St   Fax: 786-5871
Rutland VT 05701

Washington Family Court   Tel: 479-4205
255 North Main St, 2nd Flr   Fax: 479-4423
Barre VT 05641

Windham Family Court   Tel: 257-2830
30 Putney Rd   Fax: 257-2869
Brattleboro VT 05301

Windsor Family Court   Tel: 295-8838
82 Railroad Row   Fax: 295-8897
White River Jct VT 05001

Family Court Mediation Program   Tel: 800-622-6359/
Office of the Court Administrator   802-951-4049
109 State Street
Montpelier, VT 05609
www.vermontjudiciary.org/mediation

* 802 area code for all numbers

Index

Meet the Authors

Nicholas Hadden

Twenty-nine years ago Nick started his career as a VISTA volunteer providing legal aid to the elderly in Vermont. This was followed by a position as a Vermont public defender. Today, he maintains a very active St. Albans based law practice concentrating on cases before the Family and District Courts. He has handled over 2,000 divorce related actions. After hours Nick participates in the Franklin County Bench Bar Committee that works with Family Court judges to enhance the operation of the Family Court. He is also chairman of the Fairfax Planning Commission and on the board of directors of the Northwest Medical Center.

Nick graduated from Marlboro College in Vermont with a degree in international economics. This was followed by a collection of career investigations including a brief stay at Columbia University (political science) and the Sorbonne in Paris (language) before completing his law studies at Suffolk Law School in Massachusetts.

Nick is an avid tennis player and skier as well as a staunch supporter of the Vermont Lake Monsters. He resides in Fairfax with his wife, who is a silver medal winner in the Senior Olympics tennis competition and consistently beats him at tennis. Their dog prefers to remain anonymous.

Throughout his career, Nick has provided assistance to the citizens of Vermont both professionally and as a volunteer. He knows the divorce process is a "mine field" and hopes this book will help the average Vermonter locate the best pathway through it.

Cynthia Broadfoot

Cynthia has practiced law in Vermont for the past 18 years representing clients in over 1,200 divorce actions. Her law office is located in Burlington where she specializes in matters before the Family and Superior Courts. An advocate of insuring everyone's right to good legal representation, she participated in the Chittenden County public defense program for assigned council in Family and District Court proceedings. In 2003, Cynthia received the Vermont Bar Association's Pro Bono Service Award in recognition of her extensive pro bono activities. She served in an advisory capacity to a state committee developing a training program for the Family Court.

In addition to her membership in the Vermont Bar Association, Cynthia belongs to the New York and New Hampshire Bar Associations. She is also active in numerous national, state, and local professional organizations.

As a graduate of St. Lawrence University with majors in political science, English literature and Division I skiing, Cynthia is no stranger to the North Country. She received her Juris Doctor from Vermont Law School and has been a Vermonter ever since. In quieter moments her interests involve contemporary art and expanding her abilities on the piano, but she is most avid about gardening. Cynthia resides in South Burlington with her family and a bull mastiff named Emma.

John Pavese

Born on Long Island, New York, John enjoyed a wide-ranging business development career throughout Asia, Europe and the U.S. Negotiating a variety of joint venture, partnership and technology agreements with people of all cultures taught him the value of both strategy and compromise. He took early retirement in 1998 and moved to Vermont for the "better weather" where he follows his ambition to be both entrepreneur and freelance writer. John lives in St. Albans with his wife, Kathy, two cats, Tubby and Maple, and the dog, Spanky.